MO ... ..PHA MAL MINDSET STRATEGIES

Build Confidence, Stop Pleasing People, and
Gain the Power of Discipline to Become an
Assertive, Influential Leader

DAMIEN BLAKE

Before you begin...

Thank you for joining the Alpha Fam! To show my gratitude I would like to give you a FREE gift!

9 Secret Ways to Financial Independence as A True Alpha

Claim yours at www.modernalphabooks.com

Contents

Introduction

> "*The power of the alpha male comes from within, they don't rely upon external factors for their happiness, joy, and contentment.*"

Asad Meah, 2019

Do you find yourself constantly yearning for a better *you*? Surely, there needs to be more to the life that you are currently living? Are you frequently kept awake at night with the burning questions that make your balls ache and make you break out in a sweat, such as what is your purpose? And why is there *that* guy or *those* guys who seem to have everything going for them?

The good news is that you are *not* alone! You find yourself amongst the many men who want to progress up in the alphabet and be an A-for alpha instead of a B–for beta!

Are you ready to unleash your inner lion? What if I

were to tell you that this book you've picked up is the ultimate guide to unlocking a winning alpha male champion mindset—*without* being a *dick* in the process?

You, too, can transform yourself into becoming a true, influential leader without the toxic masculinity *bullshit* and bad boy alpha clichés that society is *trying* to project on you!

If you are ready to take this journey head-on with me, I would love to share *achievable* techniques in reaching mental toughness, ways to boost your confidence, and ace all the goals that your heart desires, such as:

- Women
- Money
- Success

Buckle up, dude, as I am about to take you on a life-changing journey in regaining your confidence, getting that promotion, gaining more respect, getting the girl of your dreams, standing out from the crowd, finding your *why!* Lastly, I will show you how to stop pleasing other people and realign your focus on *yourself!*

Gone are the days of wandering aimlessly at a social or networking function and not being confident enough to approach a woman that has caught your eye or feeling like you don't fit in due to society's expectations of you!

I am here to help, and my deepest wish for you is to help you reach new heights in your life by opening up your mind to a different perspective on the *modern* alpha male mindset. It is a deeply personal matter to me because what you're about to learn has brought me a financial fortune, morphed me into a desirable bachelor, and has been the catalyst that has completely changed my life for the better. Now, I want to share this special journey with YOU!

The Rewards of Being a Modern Alpha

We touched on these during the introduction chapter to this book, but surely we will not go through all the trouble of becoming an alpha male if there is not some benefit in it, will we?

Perhaps your pain was like mine, being unable to get the girl or the job. At some point in your life, you decided, "No more!" And good for you! Because too many people just stay stuck as beta males. Or even worse, as omegas.

Alpha, Beta, and Omega are, of course, letters in the Greek alphabet. As we have already shown, alphas are the most dominant and the most valued of the three— what we all need to aspire to be!

Betas lack the dominance of alphas and therefore are often seen as aggressive—generally not well-liked. The least confident of the three is the omega, who we typically equate with being the introverted *nerd* who just wants to stay at home. So, what rewards can we expect as modern alpha males?

Enterprise. You will be seen as a problem-solver, a decision-maker—one to go to when a seemingly impossible problem is to be solved. You will be known as the plan-maker, the *game-changer*. Everyone likes an enterprising individual.

Enterprising literally means to show resourcefulness or initiative! Bosses love a plan maker—someone to whom they can delegate an assignment with confidence, knowing that it will be addressed and *executed* in a way that will exceed expectations.

The reward—a resilient mentality that garners admiration from friends and frenemies alike!

Charm and charisma. You will come across as likable, *warm*, and welcoming. People will want to be associated with you and be your friend—they find calm by just *being* in your presence! In the work environment, they will know that you share your successes with others and give credit where it is due. Charisma is that X-factor that is difficult to describe, but it comes naturally to an alpha.

The reward—people love you and invite you to all their parties, trips, and social events!

Leadership. People will naturally follow your leadership style and will want to be associated with a winner. As part of your team, people will know that you have a situational leadership style with an ability to adapt to changes in the context in which you are operating.

Situational leadership is based on the theory that there can never be one leadership model that fits every situation because situations tend to differ one from the other. It also depends on the capability, maturity, and motivation of the followers.

There are apparent differences between leadership and management. Leadership is visionary; management is process-oriented. An alpha is good at both but is especially strong at leadership because of his levels of self-confidence and the levels of trust he inspires.

The reward—you will feel unstoppable; you will be seen as a leader worth following, and people will ask for you to be appointed for senior positions!

Confidence. You will be confident in exploiting new opportunities knowing that you have a balanced ability to judge risk. You will have no problem walking into a room *full* of strangers and immediately being able to make small-talk. As opposed to many other self-help books out there, I believe in actually helping you achieve this by suggesting *how*! It's pointless just telling you what the problem is without giving you solutions. That would just be counter-productive! Because you are confident, you have high levels of certainty when pursuing your objectives *and* goals.

The reward—you will wake up every morning with loads of energy and be keen to tackle any challenges that come your way!

Social maneuverability. Women will admire your natural and comfortable way of conversing with them, which is sensible and thoughtful, yet straightforward! Social maneuverability is more than this, though; it means you can adjust your level of conversation to suit the audience.

You can have a boardroom discussion, brief a group of stockholders, comfortably converse during a cocktail function and have a hearty discussion with the doorman at your hotel.

The rewards—you will be an excellent networker, moving with confidence in your social circles, having people follow you, and wanting to be part of your discussions. You will be able to get that promotion you want, get laid more often, and get invited to exclusive events, more social gatherings, and parties.

A Can-Do attitude. You will be able to handle any problem and not *shy* away from challenges that may seem daunting to others. You can harness the capabilities of people around you to support you and work with you toward achieving a common goal. You thrive on challenges—the more difficult the task, the more you relish it!

The reward—people will be naturally attracted to you and want to work with you, no matter how menial or unimportant the task!

Ambition. You will be relentless in your pursuit of personal and shared goals to the extent that it will motivate others to follow in *your* footsteps. A beta male gets distressed when it seems as if people do not have sufficient trust levels to allow him to take charge of difficult situations - this will not be you.

The reward—because you are ambitious and have set your

goals, you won't grow weary in achieving them—the car, woman, job— whatever you want!

Competitive. In pursuit of your ambitions, you will be fiercely competitive, always striving to be the best, yet ensuring that people are treated fairly. You may be known as a stern but fair taskmaster in this process, making people like you even more.

Alphas are always competitive, but they know how to harness this to the benefit of the collective. Alphas *only* compete with themselves because they have an inner locus of control. They self-validate and do not depend on others to confirm whether they are good or not.

The reward—an inner feeling of peace knowing that you are the best that there is!

Self-control. Despite your ambition and drive, you will be sensitive to the fine line between *dominance* and aggression. You will always strive to pursue your goals in a self-controlled manner, considering the impact on others. If you come across as too harsh, you will have no problems apologizing for your *seemingly* insensitive behavior.

The reward—you will feel that you have a balanced approach to life.

We have looked at some of the key characteristics of an alpha male and the many benefits that will accrue once you master the ability to be one. However, it is crucial to understand one thing: although it is beneficial to *follow* the examples of many others who have become alpha males (myself included) - you first need to find YOUR purpose, set your own agenda, goals, and then *go* for it!

Retro Alpha vs. Modern Alpha

So, where was the idea of an alpha male born? Well, the concept has been around for about 50 years but did not really catch the attention of mainstream media until the dawn of the 21st century. Before that, it was pretty much viewed as an abstract concept—not something that 'normal' guys could (or should) aspire to be.

Modern times saw it being transformed into a *real-life*, achievable goal for millions of men when. In 2005, *The Game*–Neil Strauss's bestselling book of his time in what is known as the *pickup-artist community* helped the concept become much more mainstream.

Strauss recounts in his book how he demystified the secrets to:

- Confidence
- Being well-groomed
- Having a sense of humor
- Connecting with people, and
- How to command attention in a room

His reward? He soon found himself living in what can only be described as a full-blown sexual paradise. This idea proved extremely appealing to men wishing for the same level of achievements—career, social, etc.—but primarily sexual—that seemed to be so frustratingly *effing* easy for many other men. The widespread perspective about being an alpha was "you either are, or you aren't."

The good news is that you can achieve all of this too–but only if you *truly* want to! I am a living, breathing example of that. You see, Strauss' book is what gave me the jolt of electricity–that *Eureka* moment if you will, and the inspiration. Since then, I've been paying close attention: analyzing the actions of those around me, taking an interest in the latest trends in the field, and finally, used what I've learned in practice. I have connected the dots, transformed, shaped, and sculpted that knowledge to be relevant to the current times and contemporary trends in human intersex relations.

It starts with taking a few small steps every day–one day at a time. For too many of us, thinking about changing your life seems simple, but honestly speaking, when it comes to getting your ass in gear and actually fucking doing something about it - an impossible under-taking. And for some, it *probably* is!

The key is to remain yourself, just an improved version of what you want to be! Based on what I write in this book, I am advocating that you develop a strategy for adaptation–like a blueprint for transforming from a beta male to an *alpha* male—and doing it at a gradual pace that suits YOU! Remember—it's a strategy, a *plan*! It's about making you an Atlas! An alpha male.

What Gains You Can Expect From This Book

In this, the first book in an up-and-coming series, I aim to outline how to become an alpha. In Book two, which is also due to hit the shelves soon, we will be unpacking winning strategies specifically aimed at dating!

This pilot book does *not* explicitly describe what to do to get women or to get the job you want, or how to make money. Instead, these *guidelines* I give here will benefit you in ALL spheres of life(including those mentioned above) whether you want to get something new or change a bad habit.

Some of the topics prepared for you in this book include:

- Boosting your confidence and becoming more assertive to get whatever it is that you want: the girl, the job, the house—you name it!
- Thinking like a winner—*always.*
- How to stop pleasing people and focus on yourself–respect from others will naturally follow as a result.
- Finding your purpose in life (your *why*) and standing out from the crowd.
- Becoming a subject-matter expert in communication to the extent that people will hang onto your lips.
- Differentiating between an alpha male mindset and all other society clichés. By the way, this is *not* a cheap pick-up-line book!
- Gaining a disciplined approach towards pursuing your dreams.

- Abolishing any *victim* mindset you may still harbor.
- Cultivating solid and successful habits will enable you to advance from who you are today into the *ultimate* alpha male *warrior* of tomorrow!

About the Author

Hi, I'm Damien Blake. And I am an Alpha Male!

I currently find myself in my early thirties as a successful business owner and a man with a plan—desiring to retire *no* later than my *mid*-forties! My career in corporate life has seen me progress up the ladder and also establish many thriving start-ups! My Master's Degree in Business Management and International Relations has enabled me to draw from my valuable expertise in consumer behavior and managing relations.

My diverse career path has seen me leading scores of different teams as a manager and business owner, including managing groups of people in government bodies. Today I am a charismatic people's magnet, and I've managed to embrace myself as a unique individual who does not *need* validation from others! Though I'd describe myself as being fairly talkative - I can practice *active* listening with great success! Now, when I speak, people listen—not only do they listen, but they *value* what I say.

For the past eight wonderful years, I have been coaching, mentoring, and empowering people on confidence-boosting techniques and developing schemes for becoming more assertive. I now view myself as an authority on the checklist needed for self-improvement and how to graduate to a more self-assured *alpha* male mindset! My expertise provided during in-person mentorships has already helped lots of men achieve *their* potential.

I wrote this book for *you* because I want to help men like you move away from ancient clichéd perceptions of masculinity and imprint modern alpha male methods to unlock their full potential. Trust me, I am not issuing you an impossible mission, but hey, it's up to you to accept *or* decline!

I want you to metamorphosize into the debonair, world-wise, street-smart, and captivating man you've always wanted to be - *but* you have to be prepared to put in the work because anyone can develop the qualities of an alpha male.

This is not a book that you just skim through once and then find yourself endowed with all the wisdom and balls to suddenly be an alpha male. As with all worthwhile pursuits, it takes time! There are specific tasks I've set out for you to achieve your goals.

Yes, you're going to have to put in some effort, but the rewards are well worth it (trust me, I know). So, if you are tired of living a humdrum lifestyle—just plodding along, not being successful in your sexual, financial, or work endeavors, then this book is for *you*.

Alpha - your time has come, and it's now!

The Explanation—Modern Alpha Male Mindset vs Bad Boy Alpha Clichés

Society has created some misconceptions of what an alpha male is. Many think that it is the guy who speaks the loudest, drives the flashiest car, has the biggest house, or gets *leg over* the most.

In reality, a true modern alpha does not *need* the frosting—a.k.a the *bling* and walking around like a refreshed morning rooster, all puffy chested, making a racket, because the respect he garners comes from a different source. My goal is to help you crush stereotypes and change your perceptions of what the new-gen alpha means and stands for!

The first thing I want to drive home is: being an alpha male is all about self-discipline, being in control of your emotions, knowing your worth, and always aiming to be the *best* version of yourself. All of these traits naturally build a strong leader. Everything else will follow. An alpha male does *not* compete with anyone other than himself!

You Are Your Best Friend and Your Worst Enemy

Brazilian writer Paulo Coelho writes in his book *The Winner Stands Alone*:

> *"I am my own best friend and my own worst enemy. Before coming here, I was thinking I don't deserve it, that I wouldn't be able to meet your expectations, and that you had probably chosen the wrong candidate. At the same time, my heart was telling me that I was being rewarded because I hadn't given up and had fought to the end."*

Paulo Coelho

Your mind is a powerful force that can be used, on cue from you, for either good *or* evil! It can be your worst critic (and typically is for beta males). A beta male, or *beta*, is the subordinate in a group of animals in the animal kingdom. Conversely, alpha males are leaders of these groups, and the same notion transcends the corporate world too! They are generally seen as being *real* men because they are rich, good-looking, muscular, or the boss in an organization. Betas are seen by society as submissive, weak, and relatively low in status.

The key to understanding how to be your best friend lies in understanding the critical differences between alphas and *bad* boys. Although bad boys may share some character traits with alphas, I will reveal to you that they actually have *more* in common with beta males—this we will unpack in detail in another section.

Wy Betas Are Their Own Worst Enemy

There are several things that a man needs to open his mind up to. Betas seem to struggle, and these struggles are referred to as beta-like habits. You should avoid them at *all* costs or risk becoming your own number one fiend!

Failing to appreciate *the small things*. We all want something better. Whether it be a better job, better finances, a great woman, etc., but on the way to achieving greatness, we need to stop and take in the beauty of life! See nature around us. Take a whiff of the aroma of freshly brewed coffee. Appreciate the smell of new leather or the intoxicating scent of fuel and rubber on a car racing track. Feel the rush of adrenaline pumping through your veins!

The point is; on the way to greatness, we should *never* lose sight of the small pleasures in life. If we do, then we can become materialistic, only pursuing *things* and not valuing what is unique in the world. We are holistic human beings with an overall desire to appreciate and be appreciated in return!

Not managing expectations. Chapter 2 is dedicated to setting *realistic* goals. To approach every situation with the expectation that things will turn out in your favor is *foolish*! There are things that you can control and things you cannot. Naturally, your focus should solely be on those things that you *can* control or at least influence.

The presumption on your part of everything daily to be a beer-and-nuts kinda scenario is about as realistic as barbequing minced meat on a grill—it just ain't happening! Don't get me wrong, in no way do I mean you should approach every situation with a negative mindset.

All I am saying is that you should nurture realistic expectations about the potential outcome of every engagement. When you do this, you protect yourself against possible emotional rollercoaster rides when things *don't* go as planned!

Taking things for granted. Even before the onset of COVID, people have lost things, and some individuals even grew up poor! There are countless examples of endless human suffering on this planet. Even though everyone's problems are difficult for them in their own way, you've got to take a hard look at what you *do* have in your life!

If you have a roof over your head, food on the table, a job to go to, your health, friends, and family–then you are already richer than more than half of the planet's population–and you should count your blessings and be thankful!

Being their own worst critic. An alpha seeks to take regular stock of their performance and behavior from time to time. If you don't take action in this department, then what I am trying to teach you will be pointless *AF*! Be mindful of the fact that you can overdo this like a bad fillet steak too!

Meaning that if you constantly beat yourself up and are listing all the ways in which you fail, you are destroying your self-worth! Don't scold yourself for every *small* mistake. You are human, after all! It will just adversely affect what you are trying to achieve, namely to increase your confidence.

Loving the easy way out. Nothing worthwhile is free or easy. You have to look at the long-term benefits and the effort and time it will take to manifest. What do you do when you're facing a challenge? Give up? No, if you learn to work hard toward achieving your goals, then you can handle *anything* life throws at you!

Life *isn't* fair–make your peace with it and *accept* it! Hard work and tribulations shape a resilient *MOFO*. When you understand this, you will spend less time trying to conjure quick fixes and shortcuts. I mean, be honest here; it is like constantly needing to reinvent the wheel, so you don't have to put in the effort–like all those *bullshit* diet fads! It is exhausting and an utter waste of time!

You need to determine what the root cause of your problems is and then take action against them.

. . .

They overanalyze. It is important to think matters through and plan— something I can't reiterate enough! Did you know that you can overdo this as well? Some situations require you to trust your gut and your natural instincts. But there is a fine line to ensuring that the decisions you make are not based on assumptions, and once you have done the best you can—*Decide*! No point mulling it over like a ruminating goat in your head– wondering whether you made the right or wrong decision.

Think about it like driving; when you decide you are going to drive, do it! The moment you hesitate, you put yourself in a dangerous position for a collision with another car because other drivers are unsure of your actions.

They make assumptions. Have a strong moral compass. Betas have their self-confidence rattled easily because they form *assumptions about how* the world works and how they *think* people see them—mostly based on incorrect perceptions of reality! Over time, this then becomes their new reality–their new self-limiting belief.

To prevent this, you have to rely on facts! It is becoming increasingly difficult to rely on facts when social media and fake news characterize our modern society. The best you can do is garner an understanding of how *you* fit into the world and then *suppress* the clutter as much as possible by drowning out the noise of these false prophets!

. . .

They doubt themselves. Again, part of the reason why I wrote this book is to help others with self-doubt! The aim is to guide you to unlock the *hidden* levels of your self-confidence (that you already have but have buried away). At this point, it is important to understand that as life goes on with *unrealistic* expectations—always assuming the best from every situation can also set you up for failure and disappointment!

Similarly, understanding that every situation will not always have a negative outcome is *imperative*. Self-doubt leads to low self-confidence, then leading to fewer opportunities being pursued (Woronko, n.d.).

How then do you become your own best *friend* and most useful ally, instead of you being your own best *frenemy*? There are several ways to do this—not all necessarily related to becoming an alpha male, but these are good life hacks for anyone—alpha males included:

- Enjoy your own company—Indulge in some quiet time. Do things you enjoy, like listening to music, reading a book, or just doing absolutely nothing!
- Praise yourself — *Don't* wait for others to do it.
- Realize that you are worthy—We all have many self-doubts, and we tend to think that we are the only ones that suffer from having low opinions of ourselves. But try to

understand that these are fleeting—and natural. Treat them for what they are (thoughts and feelings)–nothing more, nothing less! Don't let these shitty feelings define who you are!

- Listen to your body—Our bodies constantly give us feedback about how we may be mistreating them—being overweight, lazy, etc. Take action— if you wait too long, it all just piles up (Luna, 2020).

So much for the tricks that your mind can *play* on you! Alphas do *not* have this problem. But alphas are often associated with being so-called *bad* boys. There are some similar characteristics alphas also share with the stereotypical bad-boy beta males, like the following:

Confidence—They both display significant levels of confidence in most situations. Bad boys'—and betas for that matter— confidence levels can border on arrogance.

Rule Breaker—Both have a habit of breaking the rules. With bad boys, this may also mean breaking the law or breaking hearts and taking virginities (prover-bially speaking) - all because of that inner narcissism and belief in their *own* superiority over others! With alphas, it often means *inventing* new rules–mainly because an alpha has his own robust code of conduct, and he is bold enough to stand by his beliefs.

Strength—This can be mental and/or physical. History has shown us many characters who were physically weak but mentally strong. And the opposite, of course, also holds true. So bad boys and alphas can both be strong in either category (or perhaps both).

Leadership—They both have leadership traits, but the *key* difference is that alphas don't abuse their authority and are followed by others organically - without the need to assert dominance over others constantly!

Competitive—Both alpha males and bad boys can be highly competitive. They both want to win in all circumstances; however, bad boys want to win no matter the cost and will stoop to the lowest low to get there and get what they want - to feel they are better than others. An alpha, however, is most likely just looking for a new challenge for his body and mind, new ways to test his skills and knowledge.

Great lover—In many cases, both alphas and bad boys know how to treat their women and are great lovers. Both have an abundance of lovers over their lifetime. The alpha will achieve this by employing his natural magnetism and unshaken masculinity. On the other hand, the bad boy will use anything from displaying wealth (which he might not even have) to dark psychology bullshit to prey on the insecurities of those he wants to bed.

Dominant—Alphas and bad boys both exhibit dominant characteristics within their business and social circles. Although both are dominant, they will do it in entirely different ways. Bad boys will speak louder than those around them and make a conscious attempt to stir everything in the desired direction. The alpha male's confidence makes him dominant but in a more delicate way. He is not afraid to voice his real opinions, nor is he concerned with getting the "popularity vote. In the long-term, people learn that his decisions are made with great consideration and a cool-headed approach. These are two things that bad boy betas just *cannot* live up to!

9 Beta Male Traits That Scare Women Away

In a certain sense, as we have shown, alpha and beta males can sometimes share certain characteristics, especially when it comes to ambitious betas. They also can be confident, assertive, dominant, and great lovers – however, the inner-self of the two differs day and night! Several characteristics are unique (and by this, I mean in a bad way!) to beta males only:

. . .

Untrustworthiness — Generally, betas tend to do things only for their own advantage. They only look out for themselves and will do whatever it takes to get ahead. Being so self-serving discourages camaraderie. In contrast, alphas do things for the sake of others too. They put their families, friends, and team—their packs —as one of the TOP priorities to inspire motivation and increase trust! You see, the alpha is much better equipped to help anyone because he already took time to help himself.

E.g. In case of an emergency on the plane, you are asked to put on your own oxygen mask first and only then help others. The same applies here – many betas have sensitive heartstrings that can be pulled and manip- ulated, and they will often forget to look after themselves!

You have to note that I'm not implying that every beta is either devilish or evil! Sometimes it's just a person who doesn't know how to look after themselves and is too susceptible to the desires of those around them. Sadly they don't know their own worth and don't trust their own judgment!

Weak leadership—Beta males tend to be more indi- vidualistic. They don't know how to lead or care for others. In contrast, alphas tend to consider the benefits of their leadership style on their people and the public in general. Notably, they lead by example!

. . .

Low on ambition—Betas tend not to have the same clarity of vision as alphas. That results in them being quite narrowly focused on what they want to achieve. They are *lost* in that endless *effing* maze as they try to escape its confines.

Self-serving—Betas tend to be individualists who try to do the job themselves, also taking the credit for themselves. Alphas realize that they can only get good results through and with others. Their mantra is teamwork. That being said, an alpha does not shrug away from hard work on their own either - there are occasions where if you *want* the job done well - you have to do it yourself!

Careless—Betas tend to just stumble along without considering consequences, whereas alphas tend to be more calculating and plan ahead systematically and strategically.

Uninspiring—Betas can be very intimidating, especially toward women. Now, most women like men to be dominating. This is *not* the same thing. Betas do not usually inspire people in the long term.

Distracted—Betas tend to have difficulty focusing on any future plans, whereas alphas have no problem with

this. As far as their priorities are co
to fluctuate and drift around like a fa

sought ir
domi
ac

Lack of security—Betas do no
security in the minds of people. Their behavior is just
too damn erratic for that. Alpha males, on the other
hand, create a sense of security and safety within their
working and personal environments (Chauhan, 2016).
The alpha from your office might be intimidating at
times, but he is precisely the person you want by your
side when you are on your way to an important meet-
ing/presentation/pitch. Mainly because you know that
whatever curveballs are thrown - they will bounce right
off him.

Many of these traits coincide with each other or snow-
ball to create compound issues. For instance, since beta
males can be untrustworthy, uninspiring, insecure,
dependent, and lacking in drive and determination, they
are especially *not* ready to be inspiring leaders. Inspiring
leadership is a prime skill *reserved* for the modern alpha
male.

As an interesting aside to the point on dominance
mentioned above—a study of 118 female undergradu-
ates found that while 'dominance' was considered sexu-
ally attractive by the respondents, 'aggressive' and
'domineering' tendencies were not. In a follow-up study,
it was found that only one woman out of 50 undergrad-
uates identified 'dominant' as one of the traits she

. a partner. And here is the interesting part—

.ant is not the correct term; most women who ɹally prefer dominance use softer adjectives, like confident' (72-74%) and 'assertive' (36-48%). Not one woman wanted a demanding male–I don't blame them one bit–I mean, who has the time for a male diva? (Kaufman, 2015).

With arrogance comes boasting and an inflated status. Yet, disregarding your position does not make you *more* manly. In fact, alpha males carefully *sculpt* their image and standing, but their care does not come from a desire to be validated by anyone. It is more of a personal brand - the things he stands for.

Still, minding your status does not mean you are vain or narcissistic. Although one might think that the whole issue related to status is a function of how your brain perceives the world, it is actually much more complicated than that! It really comes down to psychology and physiology. And the main driver behind this is (*tum, tum, tuuuummmmm*)–*testosterone!*

Testosterone as a Status-Driver

Testosterone levels are often associated with levels of anxiety and/or risk. So, for instance, testosterone levels increase before high-impact sports games or other demanding physical exercises.

Testosterone levels also operate in a *positive* feedback loop. If one starts doing something and there is a spike in testosterone levels (should the undertaking be success-ful), testosterone levels *increase* in anticipation of further similar undertakings. So, suppose you are successful in eventually breaking through the barrier to speak to women at parties. In that case, the chances are that after the first time, you will be able to replicate the exercise much easier the next time!

But what are the *real* effects of testosterone on the body? First off, it is important to understand exactly what it is. Testosterone is a male hormone. A man begins to produce testosterone about seven weeks after being conceived. Testosterone levels increase through puberty and then level off. After age 30, testosterone levels tend to decrease slightly with time—a little bit every year.

When a man's body produces too little testosterone, it leads to a condition called hypogonadism. It can be treated with hormonal therapy. Testosterone affects everything in men, from sex drive to muscle mass, the reproductive system, and even bone density. It can also influence certain ways of behavior.

The body's endocrine system is made up of glands that produce hormones. The hypothalamus in the brain tells the pituitary gland the amount of testosterone the body requires. The pituitary gland, in turn, informs the testicles of this requirement. This is where most testosterone is produced, but small amounts are also produced by the adrenal glands located above the kidneys.

Low levels of testosterone may result in erectile dysfunction. Although there is therapy for low testosterone levels, it is worth noting that its use over the long term can cause a decrease in sperm production. It may also result in an enlarged prostate.

Testosterone contributes to the development of muscle size and strength. It enhances neurotransmitters, which in turn promotes tissue growth. Testosterone increases bone mass and density and allows the bone marrow to make red blood cells. Therefore, men with very low levels of testosterone are prone to more bone fractures than other men (Pietrangelo, 2018).

And what about cortisol? Cortisol is a stress hormone—*the* stress hormone! Because cortisol levels impact testosterone production in the body, it is important to keep a balanced cortisol level. Any imbalance can lead to serious health implications, causing, amongst others, fatigue, depression, and bone and muscle loss.

There is also an inverse relationship between testosterone and cortisol levels. If testosterone levels are high, cortisol levels are low, and vice versa. If you are aware of how an increase in cortisol will affect your behavior during, for instance, a party where you have to make small talk, then actively taking measures to calm yourself down beforehand can enhance your performance during the event.

It is interesting to note that these phenomena only happen if the activity you are embarking on is significant for you. If you don't have "skin in the game", then your hormone levels won't really be affected. What this expression means is that there needs to be perceived value in order for you to be invested. So, if your brother drives in a Formula 1 race that you are watching, you are likely to have a significant spike in testosterone levels, with a concomitant decrease in cortisol. But, if you have no interest whatsoever in watching the race, then you are less likely to be affected.

This is a significant first step to understand your fight or flight response whenever you are about to undertake something that is outside your normal zone of comfort. Why? Because then you can *do* something about it!

The fact that men normally have higher testosterone levels than women also explains why status is so much *more* important to men than women. Historically, a man's status has been correlated with his ability to survive via his access to resources.

What we have, how much we have, and how we use it can all play a role in elevating us on the totem pole. As a result, we are hardwired to care about our standing and success—and status breeds competition (McKay & McKay, 2015).

Simply put, when we lose during any type of competition, be it for a prize like a trophy or a woman, our testosterone levels fall rapidly, and our cortisol levels increase to prevent the same pain from being experienced again. This is also why some people are more risk-averse than others—the repeated pain from negative experiences just becomes a reinforcing circle that constantly warns, "Danger! Watch Out!"

Now that we've unpacked the problem—what can you do about it? Before you go see a GP, why not try to incorporate these lifestyle changes *first*?

- **Eat balanced nutrition**–Move away from

processed and fatty foods, and consume more whole foods.

- **Exercise regularly**—Even if it's just going for a walk to take the dog out around the block or dropping down to dish out 10 push-ups every morning!
- **Practice deep-breathing exercises** — Whenever the need arises, find a quiet spot and inhale and exhale for five repetitions, slowly.
- **Practice meditation**—This comes in many different forms; you will have to do some exploring and find a way/ways that work for *you*!

For low testosterone levels, there are also treatment options available. You may receive booster injections at a doctor or be prescribed pills. There are also many over-the-counter herbal and other medicines available. It is always recommended to speak to a doctor before you start self-medicating.

A well-balanced, nutrient-dense diet also plays a huge role in maintaining healthy testosterone levels because it assists with the overall balancing of hormones—like the wheel alignment on your car!

The two nutrients that are especially helpful for creating testosterone are vitamin D and zinc. The following foods are rich in these nutrients:

. . .

Egg yolks. A healthy source of vitamin D. Although eating too many yolks may cause problems with high cholesterol, eating one a day should not be an issue if you don't have preexisting cholesterol problems.

Tuna. Tuna is also rich in vitamin D. Apart from being linked to increased testosterone production; it is also healthy food that promotes cardiac health and is low in calories. If you don't like tuna - salmon, or even sardines, will also do. Do not take more than two or three servings per week as it may increase your mercury intake. Basically, any oily fish contains similar vitamins, but be sure to check first before making any purchases.

Low-fat milk. Milk is an excellent source of calcium and vitamin D. The best is low fat or skim versions.

Fortified cereals. Certain cereal brands, not all, are fortified with vitamin D. You may consider using these as a healthy alternative to start your day and increase your testosterone levels. Be sure to look for whole-wheat options and other alternatives that are in line with your dietary requirements/restrictions.

Shellfish. Crab and lobster also have high levels of zinc, so an occasional serving of either will do your testosterone levels some good. Alaskan king crab has

43% of your daily need of zinc in a 3-ounce serving. However, this is merely a suggestion, and if you are allergic–naturally, you will steer clear of this, or risk looking like Will Smith in *Hitch*!

Beef. A great deal has been written about the negative effects of consuming too much red meat, and a lot of it is true. Still, some cuts of beef, like liver and ground beef, can increase testosterone levels. You can also consider venison or chicken as an alternative.

Beans. Here we consider beans like chickpeas, lentils, and baked beans. They are all good sources of zinc (Pietrangelo, 2018).

Exercise is a great way to increase testosterone levels. Research shows that lifting heavier weights is the best type of exercise for this purpose. And as muscle mass increases, in turn, the body will produce more testosterone.

The best way to go about this is to perform two sets of three to five repetitions at 95 percent of your strength, aimed at the bigger muscles like the hamstrings, quads, back, and chest. The smaller muscle groups like the calves, biceps, and shoulders should also be targeted–otherwise, you will see a *Johnny Bravo* effect (so *don't* skip leg day either)

Apart from helping with increased levels of testosterone, the more you strengthen your body, the easier it is to prevent injury and speed up metabolism—a win-win situation!

It's All in the Science

The science that I refer to here is the physiological and psychological sides of a person that intermingle at a cellular level—as far as our *perception* of the world is concerned. Studies have shown that when we are in a state of (unhealthy) stress, the release of hormones related to anxiety, like cortisol and homocysteine, significantly affect the immune-, cardiovascular-, and neurological system (Yaribeygi et al., 2017).

So, when our thinking becomes toxic, it can *negatively* impact our stress response mechanisms, making us more vulnerable to disease. Researchers now believe that only 5—10% of diseases originate from genetic factors alone (Leaf, 2021). They believe that toxic stress is responsible for about 90% of illnesses, including diabetes, cancer, and heart disease.

It should therefore be evident that our mind management should be a top priority! New habits need to be formed if you want to advance to the alpha male level—not only for how you may appear on the outside but also as far as your health is concerned. Let's face it—a positive approach and exuding confidence is extremely challenging to maintain if you are unhealthy or depressed.

Studies show that global rates for depression have remained virtually unchanged from the 1990s—being stuck at about 4%. This has resulted in a large increase in the use of antidepressants which hasn't delivered *any* meaningful results.

In Australia, for example, antidepressant usage increased by 352% from 1990 to 2002 with no noticeable decrease in levels of depression, anxiety, or addiction.

Mental health issues are, of course, nothing new—there is almost daily evidence that shows that as we think, the brain changes at various levels—chemical, cellular, genetic, and structural. The important thing is that one can, and should, govern this process of thinking and not rely on pills (only).

The brain needs to be trained to think in an organized way (Leaf, 2021). In this book, I will teach you how to get rid of the baggage that weighs you down and prevents you from operating in a systematic fashion.

But speaking of *outside* appearances—on the way to becoming all you can be (as an alpha), you can make small, instant changes *today*!

5 Quick Fixes for Instant Results to Boost Your Status

Status is a function of self-confidence. And self-confidence, in turn, is a function of how we perceive ourselves to come across to others, in other words, our looks, image, and our personal brand. Apart from the tips I gave above, the following are important considerations when thinking about improving your self-worth and status quickly:

. . .

Wear the right "stuff". A lot of what we think people think about us is actually a projection of how we view *ourselves*. Whatever you wear, make sure it is the right fit. If the clothes don't fit you well, then they will not show your best side. So apply your unique style, whatever that might be, but make sure it screams *you*! Also, wear clothes that compliment your body shape.

Forget about 'regular' suits—tailor-fit is the *only* way forward! If your clothing does not meet your requirements or you struggle to find items to fit you in stores, you can use a tailor to make adjustments, and it doesn't cost a kidney either!

Related to this is the issue of colors. A study from the *Journal of Evolutionary Psychology* found that women preferred men who wore red, black, blue, and green. This may be subjective and could also be influenced by cultural factors, so it may not be the same all over the world (Schwanke, n.d.).

Also, don't wear any clothes out in public that are unironed, make you look frumpy, or have holes in them! There is nothing more off-putting than *that*!

Control your mindset. There are two ways to deal with issues: you can ignore them and hope they will go away—generally not a useful strategy—or you can make a plan to tackle these issues. Things like staying positive, focusing on remembering your *best* moments, motivating yourself, and ignoring negative thoughts are all beneficial.

Another valuable way to do this is to practice meditation. Making a plan or drawing up a to-do list can have a calming influence and a positive effect on how you feel about yourself. However, I can't stress enough that while writing stuff down and merely making a plan—they mean *nothing* if you don't take action towards them.

Posture. Pull your shoulders back, chest front—even by standing correctly, a man can immediately look taller, stronger, and more desirable! Walking around like Quasimodo with your hands in your pockets, shoulders hunched forward makes it look like you've got something to hide!

Exercise. Again, a no-brainer. Exercise makes you fit, tones your body, and makes you lose excess baggage; ergo, you feel better about yourself. It, in turn, not only influences how you think people look at you, but it also results in greater self-confidence.

A practical way to apply this is to do 20 push-ups every morning. Not only will it increase your blood flow and testosterone levels, but it will also slowly make your chest, arms, and abs more substantial—giving you a more masculine frame.

If you cannot complete 20 yet, then do whatever you can and keep increasing the number of push-ups as your strength increases. Furthermore, go for a 20-minute walk in the afternoon during lunchtime or in the morning right before breakfast.

. . .

Grooming. Presentation is important, and the first step to improving your appearance is by maintaining a high level of cleanliness. In my next book: *Modern Alpha Male Dating Strategies*, I delve into great detail about keeping your shit and junk in check! You'll find great benefits from this book too!

On the surface, this sounds logical, but can you remember the last time that you went a day or two without a shower? Ultimately, our self-confidence is influenced by how *clean* we feel and how good we smell (to other people, don't go walking around wearing the whole perfume counter, making the public choke around you).

And believe me, women like a man who smells decent, hence the proliferation in men's perfumes for sale over the past decade or two. Subsequently, if you can afford a barber regularly (at least once a month), then they will be an excellent resource, but you can also tend to yourself by learning to trim your facial hair, style your hair, and look after your skin (Centeno, n.d.).

See, you already have many tips and suggestions for improving your self-confidence, and by effect, your status. Just think—if you practice all we have unpacked until now—the *potential* benefits are enormous! Whether this is something, you must physically do, wear, seek professional help, or just go for a walk!

But we've just scratched the surface. There are two ways of becoming a true alpha! Ready to find out how?

The Two Ways of Becoming a True Alpha

I've written a great deal in this book about the characteristics of a true alpha. Now, to put these characteristics into action to become a true alpha, you should:

Be assertive. There is a fine line between assertiveness and *aggression*! As I have shown, it is scientifically proven that women do *not* like aggressive men. Yes, there may be a small category of such women, but you need to ask yourself (as an alpha male) if you are interested in being attractive to *such* women—more importantly, do *you* want to be this person?

Assertive behavior means making your mark and standing up for yourself, your values, beliefs, and needs in a respectful and nonviolent manner. Aggression is usually related to threatening or *attacking* behavior. An alpha displays his confidence without being aggressive or threatening (to himself or society).

Make people feel good about themselves. A true alpha knows that he must *instill* confidence in others, make them feel good about themselves. Now, very important here—I don't mean for you to go and pay people affirmations or compliments the *whole* time or without any particular reason! Your compliments should often come in the form of constructive feedback - recognizing someone doing a job well will encourage them to deliver the same superior standard next time.

That is what leadership is all about—winning people over. When people feel good about themselves, they radiate *positive, magnetic* energy, which also rubs off on those around them, and eventually, it sets off a symbiotic chain reaction. My point is—within this chain reaction, you stand out as the initiator—the *catalyst*! People will notice this and associate you with positive influence and *impact*.

If you do these things, there are bound to be *some* rewards.

Summary

The rewards that we mentioned right at the beginning of the book are all within your *reach*, highly attainable, and significant! Of course, for any individual, there will be *different* priorities as to the awards that they want to pursue.

Getting these rewards is not an *overnight* game! You have to be prepared to put in the hours. In the upcoming chapters, we will go into that in more detail.

You need to identify those *adverse* characteristics that can make you your own worst enemy and focus on those things that will turn you into your own best friend.

Although several characteristics make up the alpha male profile, the two most important ones are assertiveness and making people feel good about themselves. But to be able to do that, you have to understand the differences between alphas and bad boys, as well as beta traits that turn women off.

Being an alpha male is not *only* about your looks or mindset—but there is also a physiological underpinning to it. It is important to know whether your testosterone and cortisol levels are allowing you to be all that you can be. Unhealthy stress levels can lead to various kinds of diseases, especially when coupled with toxic thinking habits.

Next, we have to find your purpose...

2

The Foundation—Finding Your Purpose

The Domino Effect of Good Things in Life

In order to start on your path to becoming a true modern alpha, it is imperative to have a direction *and* purpose. A man who is focused and moving toward a specific direction is much harder to manipulate or distract than a man standing still, waiting for any semblance of inspiration.

As I said in an earlier chapter, we will focus on solutions. So, true to my word, I will explain to you *how* to find your interests, passions, and goals. But first, we need to talk a bit about the theory that underpins this. To do that, we need to investigate two closely related concepts—

1. The domino effect, and
2. Pygmalion theory

The Meaning of The Domino Effect

The domino effect means that a change in one's behavior in one area may lead to a change in other similar or related areas of behavior. It is a knock-on, or ripple effect, if you will! This happens because we don't understand that we live within a system that consists of many interconnected parts. If we change our habits or behavior in one area, it invariably leads to a change in other areas (Bose, 2021).

It is also a function of *commitment*. Once we notice a positive change and commit to this new way of behavior, the positive feedback we get from the environment gives us tremendous satisfaction. We try to reinforce that feeling consistently.

The keyword here is '*consistently*.' In this process, you develop new habits. It then becomes a reinforcing feedback loop: new actions = good results = feeling of pride = wanting to recreate the feeling = repeating it consistently = new positive habits.

What The Hell is The Pygmalion Effect?

The Pygmalion effect, also known as the "self-fulfilling prophecy", or the "Rosental effect" based on the work done by Robert Rosenthal, a Professor of Psychology at the University of California (The Pygmalion Effect (Rosenthal Effect), n.d.).

This is a psychological phenomenon that comes from the story of Pygmalion in Greek mythology. The story goes that Pygmalion, a Greek sculptor, carved a statue of a woman and then fell in love with it. He wished for her to come to life so much that she eventually did!

It is closely paralleled to the domino effect. Both of these theories simply mean that for every action, there is a reaction—positive or negative (incidentally, this is also known as Newton's Third Law). Some see it as input and output correlation. It often comes down to what you expect from the action.

It is about how you treat people and the results you get from that. If you believe people are inherently lazy and do not want to work, then that is how they will perform. On the other hand, if you show people that you have faith and trust in them, they will reward you with positive behavior. Well, in the majority of the cases, anyway!

The same applies to us—the way we think about ourselves and our behaviors. If we think we cannot change, we will not. On the other hand, if we believe we can, we need to cultivate a "can-do" environment, and it will happen in a wholly organic and holistic manner!

Remember what I said about toxic thinking and how it impacts your health? As far as habits go, whatever we think of the most manifests itself because we are giving it *energy*. Research has shown that constructive and healthy thinking (when it happens constantly and iteratively) can lead to the placebo effect, which allows the mind to fight disease (basically, you are thinking yourself healthy). On the other hand, toxic thinking can create the nocebo effect, which increases our vulnerability to disease.

It is also closely related to the abundance mentality. In recent years the waves of newly found abundance and gratitude mentality have been sweeping across the world. Most religions are based on gratitude and appreciating things in life, but most recently, authors like Rhonda Byrne (The author of *The Secret* series) have been changing the lives of many by modernizing the concepts of attraction law and Abundance mentality. It has become a mantra and a way of life for many! (Must admit - including myself)

Over the years, many of my mentees have agreed that the benefits and rewards of an abundance mentality are simply undeniable. That's great, right? Next question—what the *fuck* is an abundance mentality?

The Abundance Mentality

A well-known saying goes, *"The mind is everything, what you think, you become"* (Achor, 2015). It's *so* true! Mindset is critical to our eventual success of whatever it is that we pursue.

Quantitative research backs this up; one study conducted at Yale and Miami showed that people with positive mindsets about aging lived 7.5 years longer than those with less positive feelings in this regard (Levy et al., 2002).

This phenomenon is also looked at as a "scarcity mentality" versus an abundance mindset. Scarcity mentality means that some people view life as having a finite number of resources, like a pie. If you take one slice of the pie, there is less left for the others.

But a scarcity mindset keeps us from becoming what we can be. It limits us to think small and to think short-term. On the other hand, an abundance mindset takes the view that there is plenty out there for everyone.

On the other side of the spectrum, an abundance mentality is looking at the glass half full! For example, instead of sulking about not getting the job you applied for, focus on the fact that there are plenty more jobs out there!

So, how does one move from a scarcity mentality to an abundance mindset?

How to Transform Your Scarcity Mentality to an Abundance Mindset

Focus on what you do have. There is a saying, *"It's only when you have nothing that you realize a little was enough."* There is opportunity in *any* adversity. If you lost your job, think about the opportunities available now to find *THE* job that you've always wanted!

Instead of thinking about how few job opportunities are out there (scarcity), focus on the talents and experiences that you do *own* in pursuit of a new job (abundance). Or, if you are scared about making a career move because you may consider that you do not have enough skills (scarcity), think about all the skills that you do have (abundance) and what jobs they will be suitable for.

Even in *your* darkest hour, when *every* job application has been unsuccessful, you can use your memories of other jobs you have had before to create an inner feeling of gratitude and abundance! You can *think* of the skills (however small or insignificant you deem them to be) that you might've picked up and perfected in your previous places of employment–the connections and friends you have made, etc.

Surround yourself with those who think abundantly. Your thoughts are often influenced by those you surround yourself with. A positive mindset tends to rub off. The same thing, however, happens with a negative mindset. If you catch yourself regularly around the people who are constantly sulking over the negative details in their life, then you should consider changing your environment.

Networking and spending time with like-minded individuals will set off what I call the *popcorn effect.* When a group of people is placed in the same spot, and a few of them flourish, the others will soon follow suit! In other words - it is really important to surround yourself with "glass half full" kinda people.

Create win-win situations. Because a scarcity mentality is based on a win-lose mentality, it means that there has to be a winner and a *loser* in every situation. Rather, try to create win-win situations, both in your personal and professional lives.

Practically, it means forsaking the mindset of winning at all costs and working with someone, perhaps by brainstorming, until you have a win-win situation.

Remember, the alpha male has an internal source of motivation; he self-validates and does not *need* to win at all costs.

Include gratitude in your life. It's very difficult to feel fear or sadness while feeling grateful at the same time. Practicing gratitude is one of the best methods to improve your overall well-being—it impacts your happiness. One way to do this is to create a gratitude journal and write down five things daily for which you are grateful. It doesn't have to be complicated; you can be grateful for small things: the food on your table, the air you breathe, or the clothes you wear.

Train your mind to see possibilities. Become more aware by expanding your focus. Your brain believes what it hears, even subconsciously. What you think, you *become*! If you constantly think you cannot do something, your brain will believe this. If you don't believe in yourself, however, do you think that anything good can happen, or how do you think you'd be able to make those necessary changes in your life?

Open your mind to other options, other possibilities. Explore new ways and patterns of thinking. For example, if you are striving for financial freedom, ask yourself questions like, "If money was no object, what would I do with myself?"

Self-fulfilling prophecies and an abundance mindset go together like boobs and bras! You have to set realistic, achievable goals. Many men set life goals that do not align with their true passions and purpose.

In such cases, failure is *almost* inevitable. What you need now are the ways to find *your* purpose and passions to help you *maximize* the effects of the efforts and energy you fuel into achieving your goals!

Approaches to Determine Your Passions

Follow these steps to find your purpose:

- Find your interests.
- Find your passions.
- Identify your purpose.
- Decompose your purpose into goals.
- Narrow down your goals into objectives.

Finding Your Interests. In his book *The Art of Performance*, Jeron De Flander (2019) refers to the so-called *"Holland Code"* (classifying jobs into different categories) or *"RIASEC Interests Scales"*–which identifies six broad types of people based on their interests:

- **Realistic interests**. These people are motivated more by scientific and mechanical things and prefer to work on concrete tasks. They are also very competitive and are likely not interested in cultural or aesthetic issues.

They are the *doers*. Typical examples would be engineers or doctors.

- **Investigative interests.** Investigative people like to work with data and are analytical with the ability to organize information in a way that makes sense! They are the *problem-solvers* or *thinkers*. Examples include people in the Information and Communications Technology (ICT) industry.

- **Artistic interests.** More emotional people prefer to work with ideas and things and are very inventive. They are *imaginative* and *creative*. They don't like structure and rules and prefer to add their own creative spin on the world! They are the *creators*. Two examples include artists or sculptors.

- **Social interests.** Social people prefer to interact with others and to educate and guide people. They are the *helpers*. School teachers and social welfare workers are examples of this category.

- **Enterprising interests.** People who strive toward leadership positions and use their networking and communications skills to advance the corporate ladder or perhaps run their own business. They are the *influencers* or *persuaders*. Leaders in companies or discipline-enriched military personnel come to mind. This is probably the most common personality type amongst alpha males.

- **Conventional interests.** These people

prefer structured and orderly approaches to work and dislike disorganized workplaces. They value power, status, and reputation. They are the *organizers*. Examples include secretaries or auditors (De Flander, 2019).

We all possess an interwoven mix of these interests and characteristics, but some are more presiding than others! Our interests drive our motivation, and we should aim to pursue the goals that fit our interests.

Our interests are one of the most stable psychological constructs in our minds and are more stable than our personalities (bet you didn't know that!) To activate our interests, we need to understand that our brains desire *novelty*. We have to be exposed to things that spark our curiosity to bring our natural abilities to the fore.

But the other important part of interest activation is that of *perceived* value. There must be a reason why we care, why we are curious. If we perceive value in going for that job (higher income) or after that woman (status or sex), then our interest levels are likely to remain piqued for a long time.

To understand how this develops, De Flander refers to the so-called "Bloom Model" which shows that interests develop across three stages:

1. **Discovery**—This is the first stage where we vaguely realize that we may be interested

in something. There is still no specific goal in mind, no external motivation. Our interests need constant external activation for us to remain focused on the subject at hand! We quickly lose interest if we do not get constant exposure to these external stimuli.

2. **Development** — The second stage, during which, motivation shifts from external to internal. As the motivation becomes internal - our engagement becomes *intentional*. To move forward, at this stage, our interests require dedication.

3. **Deepening**—In the final stage, it has become our field of expertise–our passion! Now, we add a personal touch to what we have learned and we crave inspiration (De Flander, 2018). It then becomes our internal locus of control.

Now, let's deep dive into your *passions*!

Finding Your Passions. Here are some questions to help you identify your passions. If you honestly explore these, then they will give you amazing insights into your inner workings!

- What are your areas of expertise?
- What are you known for?

- What types of things do people ask you about when they come to you for advice?
- What are your skills?
- What are the unique things that make you stand out compared to others? Things that only you can do very well?
- What do you like doing? This is not the same as the previous question. What do you do when you do not have to work?
- What is your ideal job? We all have dreams but not considering income—what would be the ideal thing that you would like to do every day for the rest of your life?
- What sort of books do you read? Which genres? This will also give you an idea of the type of subject matter that attracts you.
- What is your favorite movie? And why? Why does it resonate with you? Is it the theme? The actors? The dialogue? Why can you watch it over and over again?
- When have you been the happiest? Where, with whom, when, on what occasion?
- What really upsets you? What stresses you out? What frustrates or irritates the hell out of you? What really grinds your balls?
- What genuinely makes you tick? What are some things that you do daily that make you feel alive and free?
- Who do you admire the most? Who are your heroes? Who are the people that you aspire to be like the most? And why?

These kinds of questions will help you get to the heart of who you *are* and what you were *born* to do! Now, go back to the previous section on interests and see if you can categorize what you have done here under one, or more, of the RIASEC Interests Scales.

Write down the answers to the above questions and list them under each of the RIASEC categories (each to the most suitable one). You are not allowed to *skip* any!

Is it starting to make sense? Can you see a pattern? Do you feel comfortable with your interests and passions? Don't rush this exercise; take your time (days, if need be) and revisit it again as you carry on reading this book. But as you start clarifying your passions, it is time to find your *purpose*.

Identifying Your Purpose. What is 'purpose?' Purpose is defined as a goal or a foundational principle that directs your life, and that also involves contributing to other people's well-being.

Based on the questions you answered above, you will now have a much better idea of what your purpose is or *should* be. For one person, it may be to care for little children. For another, it may be to teach children or run a publishing empire.

Still, another may have a purpose of coaching and mentoring people. Yet another may have a purpose of becoming the best surfer that they can be whilst also teaching others to surf. The point is that your purpose can be at any level of life—it is not necessarily to be the top dog in a specific organization. Yes, it could be that, but it also involves some higher achievement, of connecting to something bigger.

You see, what we want in life is *different* from everyone else's wishes, but all humans subscribe to Maslow's hierarchy of needs. Maslow's hierarchy of needs is a motivational theory that consists of a five-level model of human needs, normally arranged in pyramid form.

These needs are (from the bottom upwards)—*physiological* (food, sex, shelter, and clothing), *safety* needs (job security, safety), *love* and belonging needs (intimate relationships, friendship, sense of connection), *esteem* needs (prestige and feelings of accomplishment), and *self-actualization* needs (achieving one's full potential, including creative activities).

The point is that each lower-level need must be satisfied before you can move up to the next level. So invariably the one level is dependent on the other! So, if you get to the top—self-actualization—and one of the lower-level needs fall away, like shelter (losing your house), then you fall back to that level and ensure that those needs are met first before working your way up again.

Self-actualization needs are also known as *growth* needs. Motivation decreases as the needs from lower levels are met—these are basic needs which are also referred to as *hygiene* needs. They must be fulfilled, but they are not motivational once fulfilled!

From a purpose-finding perspective, the relevance of Maslow's hierarchy is the following: finding your passions and your purpose can only happen once you reach a level of self-actualization. This is where personal growth takes place and where true *motivation* happens!

Psychotherapist and yoga teacher, Stephen Cope gives three tips for getting the most of your purpose:

1. **Discern and know your true calling for this lifetime**. Based on the work that you have done till now, you should have a pretty good idea.

2. **Do it full out!** Give it everything you've got. This is known as the "doctrine of unified action." In military parlance, unified action is referred to as "*the synchronization, coordination, and integration of the activities of governmental and non-governmental entities to achieve unity of effort. Failure to achieve unity of effort can cost lives, create conditions that enhance instability, and jeopardize mission accomplishment*" (Unified Action, n.d.) Now, this isn't a military operation, but it doesn't hurt to approach it professionally. It needs to be a synchronized, coordinated, and integrated effort.

3. **Let go of the outcome.** The real outcome is *not* your issue. Your only issue is to determine what your true calling is and then doing it full out.

It is also important to understand that your meaning in life (your *why*) is different from happiness. The purpose is bigger! Yes, the two could intersect but not necessarily.

When people say they have a purposeful life, it's because three conditions have been met:

1. They believe their lives to be significant and worthy—So, they believe their lives matter to other people.
2. They believe they have a purpose—It is their goal or principle that guides them toward their future. It acts as a sort of force that keeps on pushing them forward toward their ideal end state, their vision.
3. They believe their lives operate in a coherent fashion—That nothing just happens randomly but that everything they do makes logical sense and is interconnected, that their lives make sense to themselves and those around them.

Deconstructing Your Purpose Into Your Goals

Goals are your passions and purpose broken down into smaller chunks that you realistically achieve instead of feeling like you have this big goal sitting on your shoulders and feeling overwhelmed as a result thereof!

Achieving goals is not just about *identifying* them. You also have to *implement* the right strategies to *action* them! If you don't, you are less likely to see them through.

This *doesn't* even have to be complex. It simply takes consistency and focus. Let's take a look at how to go about it.

. . .

Make your goals *SMART.* This stands for:

- **S**pecific
- **M**easurable
- **A**ttainable
- **R**elevant, and
- **T**ime-based

Specific. Thoroughly analyze your goals, breaking them down to the last detail and the smallest pieces possible, like hurdles in a race! Break down your goals into tasks. Lofty-sounding goals are your vision—but if you don't make tasks of them, you are less likely to *ace* them!

Break it down into manageable chunks—Monthly goals need to be broken down into weekly and daily objectives. Consider your monthly objectives to be milestones. If you just focus on the long-term goal, it becomes too daunting, and you will quickly lose focus and interest.

But if you have something that must be achieved tomorrow, it becomes more manageable. These daily objectives then roll into weekly ones, which in turn roll into monthly ones—your milestones.

. . .

Measurable. Apply benchmarks and standards to your goals and objectives (e.g., Key Performance Indicators (KPIs) to track your progress. And when you do complete the tasks associated with your bigger stage-gate—reward yourself, dude! Do something for yourself!

Attainable. Be realistic when setting your goals by completing stretch goals. This means you have to work hard at them and they should *not* be impossible! You are setting yourself up for disappointment if you set the bar too high.

And being too hard on yourself is as *useless* as a pen in a gunfight!

Relevant. Ensure your goals align with the vision that you are trying to achieve—the car, the job, the woman, whatever it is that *you* want and need.

Time-based. Apply a (realistic) time frame for achieving your goals. Nobody tries to achieve something in perpetuity. A fixed time frame serves as motivation and drive. Sometimes there is nothing like a deadline to drive you and kick your *ass* in gear!

If you have your goals set - it is time to get to work:

. . .

Make a plan. Your plan for achieving your goals needs to be formatted like a project plan. You need specific milestones, and you need to track your progress daily. Goals won't achieve themselves, and this is why a plan is essential to your success! Plus, it's a great way to track progress, you will be amazed to see that when you feel you've achieved nothing, and you look at your plan—you will see that you *indeed* made progress!

Create good habits. I will expand more on *habits* in the next chapter, but needless to say, *bad* habits can prevent us from achieving our goals. While good habits are those that can accelerate your success and enable "getting the job done" to become a part of your muscle memory—something you do *without* even thinking about it!

Show self-discipline. Discipline is key. Again, we talk about this a bit later in the book. But, this is another habit that needs to be cultivated first, which does *not* just happen overnight!

Get rid of distractions. If you want to work on your goals, you have to turn off the noise, the distractions. Be it your phone or anything else. Consider your goals to be your most important priorities and address them as such. Remember, an alpha male has his *priorities* straight.

. . .

Prioritize your work. If you have three things to do today, do the most important or challenging one first. That gets it out of the way and calms your mind. Also, the objective of setting only three goals for yourself per day will make you feel like you've been *productive* for the day.

Use the *Pareto* Principle. This is closely related to prioritization. The Pareto Principle means that 80% of your results come from 20% of your effort (Duszynski, 2021). So, focus on those relatively small efforts that will create the biggest value. A practical example is in sales, where 80% of the sales may come from 20% of the customers. Eighty percent of your personal growth achievements may come from 20% of your goals.

Embrace failures and challenges. Lessons learned may be a bitter pill to swallow, but they are very valuable. So, always welcome feedback, even if it is constructive. This should be part of your daily journal—what went well, but also what went wrong, and why, and how you can improve on this tomorrow!

Identify a mentor. None of us knows *everything*! This *mentor-mentee* relationship can provide key insights and breakthroughs when we get stuck. Finding a good mentor is an excellent idea to keep your momentum going—even if just for the sake of identifying an *account-ability* partner!

And it need not be a formal relationship, like saying, "You are now my mentor!" It could look a bit more like saying to a friend—"Let's go for a drink—I want to bounce some ideas off of you." Most people are flattered when you do this and will be willing to assist.

What is important, though, is that when you ask for feedback, you should say to the person that you don't want to be whitewashed—you want to hear an honest opinion. Otherwise, it just turns into a mutual admiration society, getting you nowhere closer to your goals, and might very well end up steering you off-course!

That being said, friends and family will often still remain biased—they *care* for your feelings and well-being, and therefore their judgment can be *clouded*! Sometimes seeking mentorship in the form of a more formal relationship can be hugely beneficial.

You can also have *multiple* mentors too! For example, when I first started my ascend on the corporate ladder, I immediately noticed that some people within the company had *exceptional* talents in their field. I have reached out to these super successful individuals (a lot of them were department heads), explaining that I would like to learn from them and if they would be willing to—I would love to have them as my mentors.

The majority (with one or two exceptions) said *yes*—those who are already successful will often be inclined to help others. After only exchanging 10-12 emails, I already had a *committed* mentor for each of the areas I wanted to improve most: sales, marketing, building a personal brand, and accelerating my career. Some of my mentors I am still in touch with and some of them I have mentored myself in a different field some years later! Today, I still *firmly* believe that my mentors have played a crucial part in my success and self-fulfillment.

If you are reaching out to a professional to try and form a mentorship relationship, make sure you research the mentor well and approach them in the most tactful and diplomatic way possible—most likely they do not get paid to do it. Therefore, *you* need to show them that mentoring you will not be a waste of their time. In most cases, it is best to arrange some periodical meetings and catch-ups. Some mentors will be very busy and will only be able to commit to a monthly catch-up, while others might be willing to commit to a weekly follow-up/catch-up.

A mentor can help you with their direct expertise, connections, advice and often even just point you in the right direction when they do not know the answer to your question. Not every person can be useful as a mentor, as not every person has the *skills* to teach others. E.g., a mechanical engineer might be the absolute best in his field, but if he is unable to describe and teach others his skills/knowledge/experience—such a mentor is of *little* to no use to you personally! If you feel like you are *not* getting what you need from your mentorship, thank them for their time and effort and stop wasting each other's time. See it as a sign to look for another mentor!

. . .

Narrowing Down Your Goals Into Objectives. We briefly touched on this before. Goals need to be broken down into objectives and even into tasks if necessary. An example of what my personal project plan looks like:

Goal	Achieve financial independence in two years.	
Objectives	**Month 1 Milestone**	Study all relevant material
Week 1 Milestone	Study Books X, Y, and Z.	Develop a mind map for month 2.
Day 1 Tasks:	Read Book X and summarize.	
Day 2 Tasks:	Read Book Y, summarize, and start with a mind map.	
Day 3 Tasks:	Read Book Z, summarize, and continue with my mind map.	
Day 4 Tasks:	Continue working on my mind map.	
Day 5 Tasks:	Complete my mind map.	

Summary

Good begets good. Bad begets bad. The Pygmalion and domino effects show that whatever type of behavior we enter into repeatedly becomes ingrained as a pattern of behavior. Our aim should be to make this a *positive* pattern!

But to do that we need to find our passions. And passions rest on interests. There are ways to go about identifying both of these components. Once this is done, you are well on your way to find your purpose!

A clear purpose is all-important for identifying your life goals and how to go about achieving them, or else you're just that lost fart in the wind! But goals may be too big to pursue by themselves. This is why they need to be broken down into more manageable chunks, namely objectives and tasks.

This is one of the most crucial exercises that you will undertake in achieving your alpha male ambitions. You, therefore, need to take as much time as possible to make sure that you do this properly.

When you have completed this task, and you step away and look at the result, you must be able to say, "I gave this my absolute best!"

However, *nothing* happens without discipline...

3

The Power of Discipline

You Are the CEO of Your Life—So Fucking ACT like it!

Imagine your life as a company of which you are the CEO. Many of us apply the world's best practice standards to our company's operations, be it in business processes, finance, human resources (HR), etc.

We also instinctively feel that all the parts must holistically work together. Though, somehow we do not apply this principle to our personal lives.

Some questions to ask yourself include:

How is your life/company performing? Is it improving all the time, or have certain areas of your life become somewhat stagnant? Are some areas underdeveloped or underfinanced?

. . .

How are you doing as the CEO of your life? Are you leading by example, or is your life just another humdrum existence?

Have you got a vision and a mission for your life? The vision says where you want to go, and the mission says how you will get there. Is it decomposed into short- and long-term goals and related plans?

How are the different areas or departments in your life performing? We said that there should be a holistic approach so that finance, HR, and operations (to name a few) all pull in the same direction. But is your health, spiritual, and personal relationships all on par and *performing* well? Or are you neglecting that side of your life and only focusing on your career?

What about your values and beliefs? We all say our company must have a value system and an organizational culture. But what about you? What are your values and belief systems?

Are you developing your life through training? On-the-job and continuous training (formally and informally) are crucial to help a company and its people grow. But what about you? Have you invested in developing yourself with formal and informal training programs aligned with your goals and objectives?

It's *all* about self-discipline! New habits do *not* get formed if we do not *apply* discipline to our lives. There are so many great benefits to self-discipline. And they are just waiting for you to discover them. So let's see what they can do for *you*!

The Benefits of Self-Discipline

Once you start on this path to self-discipline, the potential benefits are enormous! For one, your priorities are set. Muscle building is a good example—if you stick to it *rigorously*, your muscle tone will improve! Similarly, there are many other benefits to keeping your priorities and disciplines aligned:

Focus. You are more focused because you have set *achievable* goals, and you know you are working toward reaching them. It is always soothing to the mind to know that you have a plan. It may not be a good plan at first, but at least you have something in place that can always be improved - in other words, even a poor plan is a start.

Remember, when you've drafted a plan, it doesn't mean that there won't be any adjustments to it. In fact, it is an ever-evolving thing that will take shape and change as you do! So it lives with you—it is a *part* of you!

I don't know how many times in my life I have

calmed myself down by making a quick to-do list to orient my thoughts and direct my energy with a *plan*.

Decision-making. Your decision-making abilities improve because you know your priorities, and you don't let other peripheral "noise" distract you from them.

Structure to everything:

- Your life is structured better, and your perspective is more *refined*.
- You feel less guilty because you know that you are working toward achieving your goals with a plan, and you can see how the structure you've put in place for your life is starting to bear fruit. Winner winner, chicken dinner, right?
- You are taking control of your life, and *you* alone set the pace! This includes working toward attaining your goals and not swirling around aimlessly within a vortex of indecision. If you don't have a plan, you are swirling, so grab a life raft!
- You are in control of selecting which habits you want to pursue and which you want to give up. And because you govern your thoughts and your actions, you are no longer prone to *outside* influences! Of course, this is only partially true - external factors can still

have an impact, but at least you have a framework that can serve as a type of 'sieve' through which you sift all incoming information.

- You interpret life and incoming messages through this screen. The "noise" gets filtered out so important information can penetrate the screen.
- You set new and higher standards. Because you are taking a long-term stance intending to reach your goals, short-term distractions, and instant gratification *no* longer interest you.

When you do all of this, you will become a *happier* person and feel *fulfilled*, knowing the course you are on is *right* for you!

One of the major hindrances on your way to success is *you*! This roadblock you have now moved out of the way using self-discipline and a plan of action brings the following benefits:

A renewed sense of independence. You become more independent because you can control yourself much better while being more self-reliant.

. . .

Improved personal relationships. You have better personal relationships. People know that you are trustworthy, and hence it becomes a self-fulfilling prophecy in its own right—the more people trust you, the more self-confident you become, and the more influence you have.

Spare time for yourself! (I mean, who doesn't want that?) You have more spare time because you are disciplined, and you manage your available time to your advantage! You are now a more relaxed person because you do things properly and at once, therefore you actually have more time for yourself or to pursue your hobbies.

All of it sounds good and well... But how exactly do you set about doing this? It's all about creating positive habits.

Top 9 Habits to Strengthen Your Self-Discipline

To strengthen your self-discipline, you need to create new habits. I know—it sounds complicated, and all these old clichés militate against us wanting to undertake this, like "you can't teach an old dog new tricks." I call total *bullshit* on that, by the way!

You can! All it requires is a small amount of initial discipline. Here are some tips for doing just that:

1. **Start simple**—Don't try to make things too

complicated. Take small steps and work your way up.

2. **Commit to a time frame**—30 days is a good target. During that period, practice *every* day! Whether it is studying or going to the gym. Simply going to the gym three times for one week will not create a habit. Consistency is the key.

3. **Remind yourself**—Make sure that you build in reminders of sorts so that you don't slack off halfway through, especially during the first month, when the new habits are being created—these times are the hardest!

4. **Get a buddy**—Get a friend to join you in whatever the habit is that you are trying to create. It is always easier to have a buddy to support you. Make sure you choose your buddy wisely - someone who will not stick to their own goals can give you negative affirmations.

5. **Know the benefits *and* the pain**— Visualize your end goal *daily* to keep you motivated. Then think about how bad you would feel about meeting an undesired end and the consequences of returning to that state of being! You haven't come all this way to *fucking* fail now!

6. **Write that shit down**—Goals are always easier to pursue if they are tangible on a chalkboard, vision board, or piece of paper.

In fact, if you *really* want to achieve your goals, this is non-negotiable!

7. **Associate yourself with role models**— Speak to people who have achieved what you are setting out to do. Ask them for tips. You will be surprised by how helpful people are when they know you want to learn from them.

8. **Remove temptations**—If it is a *bad* habit that you are trying to break, (e.g. eating junk food or smoking), then get rid of it! Make sure you don't go to places or hang around people that will tempt you.

9. **Create a trigger**—This is something that triggers you to automatically execute a habit (e.g., for many, opening their eyes in the morning triggers a habit of checking their phone). A trigger could be almost anything so—something visual or audible, whistling, snapping your fingers, singing, getting up from where you are, or drinking a glass of water - anything that normally happens *right* before a habit occurs. It is good to know your triggers as you can try to remove triggers for negative habits and *increase* the number of triggers for the good ones.

5 Ways How to Make New Habits Stick

It is one thing to make new habits. It's another thing to *keep* at it!

. . .

First, you must have a long-term plan to ensure that you stick to the program after the first month. Consider all that I have said before and then develop a strategy that addresses the long haul—about a year is an excellent target to start with.

This strategy must have *Ends*, *Ways*, and *Means*.

- The Ends are the goals that you have set for yourself, aligned with your vision.
- The Ways are the approaches you are going to follow to ensure that the post-one-month plan remains in place.
- The Means are the resources that you will need to achieve this—time, money, etc.

Second, be consistent—this is aligned with *having* a plan! If you want to become great - potentially one of the best in the field, then you have to apply the so-called '10,000-hour rule.' This means that it takes 10,000 hours of practice to get really, *really* good at something - even if that "something" is achieving your goals or embedding *new* habits! Mind the 10 000 hour rule is of course excessive if you are talking about small habits like constantly forgetting to put the toilet seat down. However, it is a great measure for big, juicy habits and ambitions.

Consistency is the key to hone your skills and knowledge. The best of all is that when you put it in practice, it will start piling up–almost like compound interest, and before you know it, you will realize that you DO actually know your *shit*!

The 10, 000–hour rule can then be applied as the *ultimate* level of development. And with that I mean when you are willing to put in 10,000 hours worth of work, you will find, my friend, you can fucking move mountains, and this the point where it becomes a *healthy* habit that can be executed purely with your muscle memory (your mind also has a version of muscle memory)!

So, if you want to get amazingly good at something you must develop a pattern that happens frequently— the 10,000-hour rule translates roughly into two years (14 hours a day). If this still seems like a mammoth task to you, you can divide it even further down into the number of hours a day that works for you. For example, if you had to prolong your plan to four years, it equates to roughly 7 hours a day, and if you draft a five-year plan, you are looking at approximately six hours a day. After 10, 000 hours you will undeniably be an *expert* in the field!

Sure, it might take longer, however, it means doing it at your pace! Bear in mind, your aim is to become a subject-matter expert in this, not just "good" at it! You are already good–you want to be *fucking* awesome!

By the way, this point about having a plan is a recurring theme throughout this book, as we also showed in the previous chapter. Everything needs to be underpinned by a plan. Or else it is just knee-jerk short-termism that serves you *fuckall* purpose!

Third, be patient. Patience, by itself, is also a habit! Most people expect the results from trying new habits to be visible *immediately* (there's that instant gratification thing again), or for them to be able to do what they aspire to do within a month or two. If this does not happen, they easily fall back into their old habits because they could not see it through with patience!

Fourth, track your progress. In business, one implements a system based on KPIs (Key - Performance - Index) to track how the business is performing—daily, weekly, monthly, quarterly, and annually. The same applies to the discipline that you need to bring to the table with your new habits.

Track your performance on a daily basis against a set of KPIs and record your performance. Try to formulate both qualitative and quantitative KPIs. So, if your new habit is to break out of your present depression levels and meet new people, a quantitative KPI could be the number of new people met at the social club, golf club, etc., per week or month.

A qualitative KPI could be the amount of knowledge you have gained during your discussions with these people. This cannot *really* be measured, but if you journal the results of these conversations, you will soon start to see how you are growing in terms of your own knowledge base!

Fifth, make sure that you use a *carrot-and-stick* approach to getting to your habits. There needs to be rewards and reprimands. Each newly-formed habit is an occasion for celebration. If you are studying and you have applied yourself during the week, then give yourself a day off as a reward and a way of celebrating a productive week.

As far as reflecting on your mistakes and failures is concerned, be careful that this doesn't become an excessively self-critical exercise, or else you are likely to start *fucking* with your KPIs in a non-sexy way to prevent significant pain.

You need to take notice of what went wrong and also forgive yourself in the process. Failures are an inevitable part of our lives, and they *will* occur! So, if your new habit is healthy eating but you have snacked on fried chicken, tell yourself the consequences of this, maybe by weighing yourself, and then decide how you are going to ensure that it does not happen again.

It is all about the long-term: one meal of fried chicken won't make you fat– the same as one gym session will not make you fit. If you ever slip–*accept* it and make sure you saddle the horse immediately the next time, get on it, ride it hard, and put it away wet!

Reward all your gains and *learn* from your failures!

Using Disappointment From Past Lessons Learnt for Motivation

When we disappoint ourselves, we tend to dwell on it. On the other hand, research shows that people who forgive themselves (who have elevated levels of self-empathy) seem to have less of a problem with this (Cutruzzula, 2020).

And as I said earlier—*shit* happens! There will always be disappointments and failures. The trick is to get *over* it. Here are seven tips that I've found to work for me.

Accept the situation - Accept what went wrong so that you can get over the sense of *shame and disappointment.* This is also how one gets over grief. I'm not saying you should be emotionless and just move on. Sometimes you may need to sulk too - without accepting our negative emotions, we can never truly embrace the positive ones.

I have a kind of a rule for myself - if I have been truly down for some reason and feel like I can no longer keep going, I allow myself a day to feel upset. On that day, anything goes - binging Netflix, comfort foods, most likely completely ignore all messages, calls, and emails. In my eyes, it is a reset button - a time to empty and then recharge my mental battery. I have only one rule in this matter - the day after, I MUST get up and continue the grind - I take a step back and start approaching the problem again, trying to see some overlooked solutions. Most of the time, the solution eventually presents itself.

Whatever your process is -that is fine, dude—remember to always DO YOU!

Don't forget to do introspection to find out *where* things went wrong. A simple trick is to state to yourself what went wrong aloud and why you feel the way you do or write it down. Something like, "I'm really disappointed in myself because I did not achieve Goal X."

Just doing this will bring a sense of relief and clarity, and you may find that it really was *not* a big deal after all —not in the grand scheme of things, considering your long-term plan!

Don't treat yourself like an enemy. Rather, treat yourself like you would your friend if they came to you with a revelation about how they have failed at something. You are not likely to be judgmental, so why be that way to yourself? If you treat yourself in the whole situation like a good friend, it can help you to *not* playing the blame game!

Also, this is where the value of having an ally in your new habit-forming process is so vital. Either you can vent to this friend, or you can jointly decide what went wrong and how it may be remedied.

Acknowledge that you have big expectations. Recognize that this is a challenging process and that you will fail sometimes. Be realistic about the goals you set and understand that such goals are difficult to achieve by their nature. But here is the thing—doing things the same easy way as we've always done is *not* going to make us reach our goals!

Do something different. It is sometimes valuable in times of stress to do something you haven't done before to take your mind off the situation. Do something different (but healthy). Binge eating or drinking is *not* a healthy distraction to use regularly, and it may even become a terrible new habit! Call up an old friend. Go for a brewski, or have a barbeque. Take a walk if you have to. Understand that this *isn't* the end of the world!

Learn the lesson. To do this, you need to ask the *right* questions about what went wrong so that you can learn from it and not repeat it next time. So consider whether you've set reasonable time frames for that goal. Did you prepare properly beforehand? Did you ask someone knowledgeable for their assistance?

Doing this will help you get to the bottom of the issue. A good tip is to use the so-called "Why-Why" technique. You ask, "Why did this not work?" Maybe the answer is that "I was ill-prepared." Then you ask again, "Why was I ill-prepared?"

The answer could be that you did not read up on the subject. Then, you ask why *again*! You carry on with this exercise (listing at least six "whys") until you get to the root cause of the problem. But to just say, "Oh, I suppose that just didn't work out for me" is *not* going to do you any good!

. . .

Recalibrate. You need to adjust so that you don't repeat your mistakes. Don't generalize and say, "I'll do better next time." Let's not beat around the bush–you *won't*! You have to be specific with your plan of action in order to prevent the same issue from occurring.

Understand that you care. You would not be so disappointed in this outcome if you were *not* really committed to making it work. This means it is important to you, which is a good thing because it shows your passion. And remember–passion is what fuels your traction!

My Personal Strategy - Start Your Day Properly!

I would like to share my personal morning routine with you to give you an insight into how a plan/strategy looks like when adjusted to an individual. Developing and sticking to new habits is challenging to say the least! It is easy to backslide down a toxic hole of negative thinking if you let your mind wander. When we wake up in the morning, our mind is in a vulnerable state as it starts reorganizing itself and thinks about what is going to happen for the rest of the day.

It is crucial to maintain your self-discipline and focus on reaching your goals and forming new habits to regulate your thinking from the *moment* you wake up!

I follow this routine:

- I write down any thoughts that come to my mind when rising during the first 90 seconds or so.
- Next up is my focus on the task to conquer the day. To direct my thoughts purposefully, I go through the following "checklist" in my mind:
- I am making a conscious decision to regulate my thinking to focus on my goals –I will boost my intelligence levels in a *positive* manner, and I will do what it takes to pursue my goals.
- I *will* remain in control of my emotions today —they belong to me and are therefore mine to control! This includes removing any anger from my life, placing a guard over my mouth, and thinking *before* I react!
- Today, I *choose* to set my mind to the happy switch! Stress will work *for me* as I banish the beta mindset! I will also help someone today because it makes me feel good about it!
- I *know* that the pursuit of my purpose and related goals are long-term exercises. I will *maintain* focus on my end goal.
- I then dish out some pushups to get the blood flowing and energizing me, followed by a big healthy breakfast.

Reaching the alpha male end-state is a mentally *tough* process! Using the techniques, I described above will help you build your brain and develop mental resilience.

Over time, it will become second nature, but initially, you have to force yourself to go through the process, even if it feels unnatural at first!

Summary

It's amazing how we always apply our minds to our career goals in a professional way but refuse to do this when we have (or want to have) personal life goals to pursue. Those goals can arguably be even more important! Generally speaking, this is due to a lack of self-discipline. To achieve goals of this caliber, the power of discipline is an *absolute* necessity.

One of the main ways to cultivate good self-discipline is to create positive habits and make them stick! As I discussed, there are many techniques to do this, and you need to calibrate your brain toward positive thinking first thing every day.

Also, despite your best efforts, there *will* be failures. The point is to learn the lessons these failures present and utilize healthy practices and avenues to get up, dust yourself off, forgive yourself, and move on with your journey toward improving your self-confidence and mental resilience!

4

The Self—Confidence Is My Middle Name and It's the Key to My Success!

What is confidence all about?

- **It's your ability to believe in yourself.**
  This might be knowing that your idea at work is a great one, feeling that you can do something, or understanding that you can ask a girl out without backing out of it.

- **It's about understanding yourself and having self-acceptance.** This is when you have no desire to fit in with the crowd when you *own* your sexuality, sense of style, or haircut – everything about the real inner self as well as being freaking proud of who you are!

It also *doesn't* imply that you are an extrovert or an outgoing person. You can be self-assured but be somewhat reserved–it doesn't mean that you are not confident about yourself!

Self-Worth and The Importance Thereof

Why is self-worth, also known as self-esteem or self-confidence, so important? Firstly, it is *vital* to understand that self-worth is all about what you think about your values and worth. It is a highly subjective experience that determines whether you feel worthy *or* unworthy! It also shapes your perception of how others see you and your personal brand.

Your self-esteem is linked to how you feel and think about yourself. Your level of self-worth bears an impact on things like:

- The like and value you have in yourself.
- How much you believe in yourself and the things that you are doing daily.
- Your ability to stand up for yourself when the need arises.
- Your willingness to try new things or things that you perceive as challenging.
- The ability to move on, without *damning* yourself unnecessarily.
- The belief of you being good enough and actually mattering in the universe and to yourself.
- The ability to believe that you deserve every happiness in the world!

When you possess a high level of self-worth, the way that you perceive and feel about yourself is much more likely to be positive. On the other side of the spectrum, if you have a low level of self-esteem, the chances are that you don't feel good about yourself and think about yourself negatively—making it less likely for you to stand up for yourself!

Self-worth also directly impacts a person's motivation. A person with high motivation tends to pursue opportunities more readily and more forcefully than someone with a *low* level of self-worth. This makes sense because if you *think* you have little value, then you will also truly *believe* that your chances of getting that good job, or that great girl, are low!

Because self-worth is labeled as an *abstract* concept, it is difficult for people who don't have high self-worth to gain it—but *not* impossible! It usually starts when you are a youngster—children who are raised to have high levels of self-worth tend to make better decisions later in their adulthood phase.

One factor that can impact both your self-esteem and confidence is the people you decide to invite into your life! Especially when it comes to your friends.

How Self-Esteem Relates to Confidence

When you have a high level of self-esteem, you feel good about yourself! It is only human and natural that when something happens that knocks your confidence, you tend not to like yourself very much in those moments.

Let's face it, we all feel like this sometimes, but when

we feel like this for a long time, it can become problematic! It doesn't matter what the origins or source of these things are that negatively impact your self-worth and confidence; it's imperative to remember that you have a *fucking* right to feel good about yourself! That is why I am here to help you find a way!

Naturally, as we males are—a big part of where we want to be confident is on the dating scene, so I want to briefly touch on it, based on some studies that were conducted. This information aims to show you how confidence is good, but how overconfidence and being too self-assured can go both ways.

The Science Behind Confidence When it Comes to Dating

A study conducted by Murphy showed that being a bit overconfident may not be such a bad thing—but that you should avoid coming across as arrogant (Murphy, 2015). How did he arrive at this finding?

He conducted four studies to determine what makes confidence so attractive. He also wanted to test the hypothesis that people could gain a "romantic upper hand" by being overconfident. His rationale was that overconfident people (who have a highly subjective *positive* view of themselves) might act in ways that parallel signs of genuine confidence.

During these four experiments, Murphy measured participants' confidence in a variety of ways:

· · ·

Study 1. A group of opposite-sex participants had to rate the dating profiles written by another group and then had to rate the authors on a number of positive qualities. Participants who came across as unabashed were also highly rated on their dating profiles–so it seemed as if there was a strong correlation between confidence and romantic attractiveness.

However, overconfident individuals were, in fact, not seen as more attractive, which led the researcher to theorize that self-assertiveness might have a *negative* impact on desirability as a result of some unknown measure— perhaps arrogance? Which in such cases offsets the benefits of confidence!

Study 2. Participants had to rate dating profiles for arrogance in this study, and the study leaders' thesis was found to be correct—overconfident participants were perceived as being attractive but more arrogant! So, it seems that confidence and arrogance balanced each other out with the result that blustering people were neither better off nor worse off romantically due to their inflated self-worth.

Study 3. Here the individuals were asked to target a member of the opposite sex who was sitting at a table with a self-assured person. It was found that people were less willing to compete with overconfident individuals and would rather look for another person to chat with.

This suggests that arrogance (despite being unattractive), when combined with confidence, was a powerful deterrent to any would-be suitors. In plain language—if a male sees a woman sitting at a table with a man who seems confident and arrogant—although there may be no indication of a romantic relationship between the two, our *bachelor* would instead look for someone else. While being confident—you will sometimes automatically remove a lot of competition without even knowing it!

Study 4. The same deterrence effect was repeated when money was on the line. Even with monetary incentives, participants were not keen to compete against overconfident profile individuals, while overconfident participants were willing to compete at all levels. If our would-be suitor is too self-assured (and hence arrogant), he is not *likely* to be deterred from going after his prize.

In line with the findings in Study 4, a final simulation study showed that as levels of competition increased, the negative effects of arrogance on romantic success decreased, while the positive effects of confidence increased.

So, as I said in the opening paragraph of this section— what these scientific studies revealed was that confidence is a highly prized commodity when it comes to relationships. Even being a bit overconfident might be valuable - as long as you don't come across as a complete douche about it!

Keeping healthy levels of confidence comes down to an understanding of possessing both masculine as well as feminine energies and how to use them to your advantage.

The Yang and Yin of Masculine Energy And Its Applications in Your Daily Life

Did you know that both males and females have at least a little bit of both masculine – as well as feminine energy? Ancient Chinese wisdom also refers to these as Yin and Yang energies! A strong masculine energy that you possess can help a woman feel more feminine. In the same way, a feminine woman helps a male feel more like a man!

Having said that, alphas take the best advantage of their masculine energy as they ooze this, and it is what makes them attractive and magnetic to those around them, including women. Even the manliest men on earth actually possess both energies. But the key to unlocking self-awareness is a MUST for the path to alpha-dom!

None of the energies are linked to any gender in particular! Yin bears reference to the feminine energies in life, and Yang is the masculine ones. For example, when you give—this action is associated with the masculine (Yang), and receiving is an action associated with the feminine (Yin). When we have a healthy balance of both of these divine energies, we feel at peace with ourselves! Even though this seems like a simple enough task—it is, in fact, very hard to achieve!

Not one person will ever maintain an optimal balance of these energies, but comprehending what they are and knowing what you can do to balance the scales, can help you feel more harmonious with yourself! We all have either a dominant feminine or a dominant masculine side.

These energies feed off one another and balance one another out! There are four types of Yin and Yang energies, and they are categorized as follows. (I've listed them for you from the most masculine to the most feminine of combos):

The *Greater Yang* - This is the most masculine of divine energies.

Characteristics

- Assertiveness
- You are goal-orientated
- Natural-born leader
- Problem-solver

Strengths

- You don't experience burnout often.
- Mind-over-matter is your game!
- You don't get sick often.
- High energy and drive.

Polarity

- You can reach boredom easily.
- People are intimidated by you more often than not.
- You don't give yourself enough credit for what you bring to the table.
- You give too much to others (very little to yourself) and don't receive often enough.

Re-calibrating

- Grow your strengths as best you can to how it suits you and not the other way around!
- Learn to delegate.
- Inspire others by being yourself and leading by example.
- Avoid feeling let down by others or disappointed in yourself.

When you can balance these four energies, you will radiate a certain magnetism that will make everyone around you drawn to you (females included) and can use this to your advantage. Plus, you will feel great about yourself!

When you understand yourself and how to recalibrate your energies, this will instill a renewed sense of confidence as an alpha male. However, there are certain things (no matter how confident you learn to become, that alphas just do not do!)

. . .

The *Lesser Yang* - This is the first energy in the dominant masculine energy level. These individuals like a faster pace to life and are predominantly extroverted.

Characteristics

- Open-minded and kind-hearted individuals.
- Higher expectations when it comes to what they want out of life.
- Ability to dream big, but can be objective and realistic at the same time.
- You don't get upset easily.
- Ability to look to the future and ace goals.

Strengths

- People want to be around you.
- You always seek new ways to grow and learn.
- You can recognize the good in people and in every situation that comes your way.
- You strive for a perfect work-life balance.
- You like to dabble in many different things and don't find gratification in focusing on just one project or one interest.

Polarity

- Sometimes you are overwhelmed by your energy.
- A propensity for anxiety.
- When things do go your way in life or in a relationship, you become stagnant and find it

too peaceful and might even *sabotage* the happiness thereof!

- Often you might overlook your blessings and be ungrateful of them.

Re-calibrating

- Satisfy your curiosity as often as you can!
- Make a yearly, monthly, weekly, and daily wishlist and do everything you can to accomplish them and make it become your reality!
- Take care of yourself by doing the things that make you feel good about yourself.
- Learn to say *no*! No to people, and no to social engagements or other things that may stand in your way.

The *Lesser* Yin - This is when you are somewhere between 60 to 80 percent Yin and between 40 to 20 percent Yang! (Nuur, 2018).

Characteristics

- You feel in harmony with yourself most of the time.
- Curious and creative, but less analytical.
- You are more of an introvert than an extrovert.
- Enjoys the process of discovering yourself.
- Things are done at your own pace, and you might take slightly more time than others to

complete it.

Strengths

- You are seen as a *safe* space everywhere you go!
- Others can be themselves around you– without the fear of judgment.
- You stand up for others when they can't/don't stand up for themselves–but not so much for yourself!

Polarity

- A tendency to turn both cheeks for a beating sometimes.
- You sacrifice a lot of yourself.
- A natural inclination to create narratives in your head that do not always exist.
- You have a hard time letting go.
- Quick to jump to conclusions and assumptions.

Re-calibrating

- Indulge in creative activities–make time for yourself to do these things.
- Do some "me" time, take care of yourself in the way that matters the most to you and makes you feel good.
- Give back to others.

- Set boundaries for yourself and other individuals.

The *Greater* Yin - This is the most *feminine* of divine energies! It is all about senses, nighttime, creativity, and feelings.

Characteristics

- You might not be an introvert, but you possess dominating, introverted qualities.
- Others have possibly called you needy or sensitive on previous occasions.
- You prefer your alone time over spending time with others.
- You feel everything!

Strengths

- You possess integrity.
- Transparency and honesty.
- Ability to connect with people or situations profoundly.
- People gravitate towards you because you make them feel special.

Polarity

- You bleed people dry like a sponge.
- Your feelings are hurt easily.
- Tendency to feel alone and isolated.

Re-calibrating

- Meditation.
- Journaling.
- *Feel* those feelings.
- Create time for yourself daily to process and work through these emotions.
- DO YOU! (cry, scream, dance–do whatever you need to do to restore balance).
- Help someone out. This will restore your power and make you feel good.

Why Would I Want To Enhance My Masculine Energy?

If you feel stagnant, uninspired, and unmotivated, it may be due to a lack of that very same masculine energy. Developing *positive* masculine energy means getting the confidence to make decisions and then taking action. Confidence comes from two sources:

- Trusting your feelings, and
- Positive feedback about past experiences as a result of actions that you took.

The sequence of masculine energy. It is the side of you that is responsible for *taking* action! It is a function of how you think, decide, act and the result of your actions. Sequentially it works as follows:

1. Confidence
2. Decision
3. Action, and
4. Result

There are three different types of masculinity, and they can be categorized as follows:

Positive masculinity. Positive masculinity endorses being in touch with and understanding your feelings. Therefore, the core of masculine energy is *action*— remember the sequence we spoke of earlier? To do this, we need to calibrate our mind as an *instrument* to analyze our emotions, come to a decision, and then take the appropriate action. But even if you have the objective in mind and the resources too - you still have to put it into practice!

Negative masculinity. The opposite of positive masculine energy is–of course, *negative* masculine energy. In this case, your mind has a surplus of will but insufficient desire to act upon it! When someone operates in such a mode, they are hell-bent on undertaking what they have decided *without* thinking about how the consequences affect them or others.

Negative masculinity does not embrace the process of "listening to feelings." If it does not like what it is perceiving, it rejects it because such feelings may be seen as too intrusive–too problematic! The core of negative masculinity is selfishness. Typically, these people come across as not wanting to share feelings and actions with their partners or demand everyone to buy into the way they decided things should be done.

They then try to imitate the behavior without understanding exactly what it is that they are doing. You often find this in people who try to sound authoritative on a topic, but you can tell that they have no idea what they are talking about–this is both hilarious and ridiculous at the same time!

Have you ever had a manager who always seemed to remind everyone *constantly* that they are in a position of power? The one that decided that micromanaging everyone and dishing out disciplinary meetings and documents will assert their authority?

Welcome to *negative* masculinity–the need to assert *dominance* over others just to try to feel better about yourself or hide incompetence. Another good example would be petty attempts to demonstrate authority by those who are loathing power but do not have it–e.g., an office clerk who will not accept a document because you were two minutes late and they are now "technically closed" for the day or a college security guard that kicks you out of the campus because you forgot your student ID at home even if you have a picture of it on your phone. I am sure you have had your share of the little men, desperately clinging to the scraps of power in their life...

. . .

Mock masculinity. Mock masculine energy is when someone develops their masculine side but at the same time does not understand how the experience really works. It is almost as if they are acting out their masculinity based on the example of someone that they have seen and admired. A bit like a parrot mimicking the words it has heard without any understanding of the meaning.

Assertiveness and Dominance without Hostility

Being assertive and knowing what you want is not the same as coming across as belligerent and hostile! And you should know the difference. It is all about saying what you want in a confident and not in a *small-dick energy* manner! In other words, how to be assertive without being an aggressive asshole about it.

- Be clear about what you want, and if you need to relay the message, do so in a firm manner without being demeaning or manipulative about it.
- When you speak, maintain eye contact at all times.
- Keep an upright and straight posture.
- Make sure that your research and homework are done before you engage!
- Take a time out if you need to.
- Do not play the blame game!
- Maintain your coolness! (After all, you are damn cool, literally!)

10 Things A Confident Alpha Wouldn't Do

This is the part where I really want you to start feeling that you are well on your way to becoming the alpha male that you desire and aspire to be!

When you can get to the point where you are confident in the alpha staring back at you in the mirror, you feel good, and every damn facet of your life gets better! Although you might feel that you are not there yet, it is definitely something that you can develop and then build on, every.freaking.day!

Sure, confidence is super important, but hell–there is a list of ten things I want to share with you that confident alphas never, ever do, no matter what!

They never put other people down. This is a characteristic that is reserved for beta males! You should not be shunting other people down or belittle them in order to derive some sort of sick pleasure and make yourself feel better in the process. They think that by being this way, they are superior to others.

The alpha way–Inspire people and help guide them on the right path, including how to also be an alpha!

Note: It does not mean you will never upset people. It simply means that you should never aim for that to be the end goal - every alpha has to burn some bridges here and there as he moves through life.

. . .

Alphas do not feel the need to boast or brag. This is a complete "boner killer" for anyone around you, especially when it comes to the ladies! Do you think you will succeed by posting shirtless pictures of yourself with a few hotties on the beach? The thing is, confident men or alphas don't *need* to! Don't even get me started on the men who wear massive brand logos on every piece of clothing.

Alphas don't need admiration by telling everyone how good they are–because everyone else already knows they are dope as fuck!

They have no need for validation. Alphas don't need an "atta-boy" from those around them, because they are self-aware and self-assured.

They are completely at peace with themselves and feel comfortable in their well-moisturized skin.

Confident men don't let themselves go. They take care of themselves, including moisturizing their skin!

Alphas are not afraid to take care of themselves, and they are fully aware that it is good for them to be this way! So yes, they are not afraid to sleep on comfortable sheets or use Pink Himalayan scrub salt to exfoliate.

They know that by taking care of their skin, they automatically feel good about themselves. I mean, have you ever tried it and felt this experience for yourself? If so, you will be able to relate–if not try it!

· · ·

Alphas are not overly "thin-skinned" or "fragile". A confident man can take and accept constructive criticism. And no, it might not be nice to hear, but they look at it from the point of how they can use it to their advantage to benefit them!

Confident men can hear it, take it and then apply it in the correct manner.

Confident men don't apologize all of the time! Many of you might be struggling with this, but it is a sign of insecurity! You are not a bar of chocolate, so an alpha's mission is not to please everyone.

Alphas are not insecure, nor do they go around apologizing and feeling uncertain about themselves.

They don't sit around and wait for shit to happen for them or to them. *A confident man is fully aware that he needs to go after what he wants. Alphas know that they are in control of their destiny.*

Alphas don't have time to engage in gossip–I mean seriously! *A confident man does not have time to sit around and talk shit about other people. Alpha's are too busy kicking ass wherever they go to engage in such menial bullshit!*

They don't avoid eye contact. *An alpha male knows that it is important to establish and hold eye contact when talking* *to others. Confident men don't avoid it or look intimidated and scared when they talk to people!*

My personal favorite–Stalking other people on social media. This rings true, especially if you don't want to be branded a creep when it comes to women. Alpha males have a ton of other shit to do than waste time on this!

The next thing we need to unpack is understanding how to face your fears, now that you have confidence and know what *not* to do.

Facing Your Fears

In situations of dispute, alpha males *face* their fears; they don't run from them! This is what's at the epicenter of every beta male—self-inhibition and passivity. Fear comes in different shapes and sizes. Before we move on to the four types of fears that all guys have to face, let's look at the oldest fear of all—approaching *the* girl! If you are a beta male, you will think of all the things that can go awry. You then let go of the idea because you are shaking in your boots.

Again, this becomes a self-fulfilling prophecy because when you have a similar opportunity with another woman next time - You back out due to the same fears and insecurities! Now you have fed this seed of fear. Over time, this seed is watered and eventually becomes a *monster* that consumes your feelings and neutralizes the sequence of positive male masculinity that should lead to action!

Your fears become all-consuming, and before you know it, they make it impossible for you to make any move on *any* woman. In this insane situation, this giant tree has grown from a *small* seed. Yet, the fear never really existed; you just fed it and *relinquished* your power!

So, alpha males *don't* act this way! They overcome their fears by taking immediate action. Not in an arrogant fashion but in a confident one—even if they have the same insecurities in the back of their minds. Eventually, their insecurities become weaker as they become more successful at overcoming their fears.

Part of overcoming your fear is to be assertive. As in dealing with conflict, you have to stand up for what you want—for what you believe in—confidently, not aggressively (for the reasons we have discussed before). Not passive because that may make women question your ability to protect and provide. Be *assertive*!

As for the four kinds of fear that we mentioned earlier, they are the following:

The "I shat my pants" kind of fear. This is a legitimate fear for your life. There are many categories of this: hunting, a violent sport like boxing, or perhaps going to war.

My personal experience has also taught me that an element of this type of fear is *essential* for personal growth—to move out of your zone of comfort. I'm not advising everyone to take up a gun and go to war, but do something that is *outside* of your comfort zone. Maybe mountaineering or skydiving. The adrenaline rush makes you feel alive! And the more often you do it, the more you get used to it. But most importantly—the more your confidence grows!

Fear of failure. We touched on this before, but many people don't fulfill their potential because they are afraid of failure. This is not the alpha way! Do what needs to be done despite your fears and insecurities. In the moments of doubt, I often remind myself of the following mantra: "It's better to regret the things you've done, rather than the things you haven't".

You see, when you are constantly afraid of failing, you might miss out on great opportunities. Instead, you should approach it by learning when the time is right to take a leap of faith as well as when and how to utilize the right strategies to get you there!

As previously mentioned, approaching the woman is a good example. Spend time convincing yourself to do something. It is courageous and necessary. Face your fear head-on and refuse to let up until you come out victorious on the other end of it!

The fear of taking responsibility. This is a bit of a tricky one. In this context, I mean that there is a time to be a hero and a time not to! The best approach as an alpha is picking your battles and picking them right!

Some battles you will win, and some you will forgo. You need to know which ones you are best armed and prepared for, and willing to face!

The FOMO! I really like this acronym because there is no other way to describe that feeling accurately! In the case of beta males and boys - they are willing to do anything—and I mean the irrationality knows no bounds in order to avoid feeling left out or missing out on something. You see, the difference for the alpha male is that he is too zen with himself to succumb to the Fear Of Missing Out! Why? Because he has a direction and an abundance mindset!

Talking With Actions—Reaction vs. Response

An alpha is immersed and is fully aware of what is happening around him. He is, therefore, more confident about his actions. His secret? The alpha male understands the difference between response and reaction intuitively, which makes it a great source of confidence. In the previous section, we spoke about fear and how to relate to it if you are an alpha. Now, an alpha knows that although response and reaction sound very similar—when you are in a stressful situation, the difference between responding and reacting is telling. It may mean the difference between winning and failing—between breaking a relationship or *enhancing* it! Even the difference between losing your job or getting a promotion.

The difference between the two lies in a deep

breath, a pause, or a brief moment of mindful presence! That moment can mean the distinction between sending the entire situation or relationship soaring to greater heights or falling down a slippery slope.

Let's take a closer look at what the words 'respond' and 'react' represent and learn some tools to help you respond to life's circumstances. Even when it's brought about by stress, we want to address it in a way that best serves your wellbeing and everyone around you.

Reactions—*Reactions are instinctive.* Acting with your primal brain. Doing something without thinking it through first—not considering the implications! Pretty much like how an animal reacts to an external danger stimulus—it activates an immediate fight or flight response.

Responses—*Responses are considered.* It means you first think through what the potential implications of your actions could be, meaning considering the pros and cons of your words or actions. You observe first, and then you orient yourself to what these stimuli are coming at you truly mean. In other words - *you strategize!*

Some of the many methods and techniques out there can help you set *new* default settings in your mind! Instead of emotion and *impulse-fueled* reaction, you will be able to make calculated, thoroughly thought through responses – *always* helping you maintain a strong position and make the most favorable decisions to serve your purpose.

I will present you with a few of these methods, and you can mold your own strategy that will best suit your situation.

- **O**bserve
- **O**rient
- **D**ecide
- **A**ct

This is known as the "OODA Loop." This is a decision-making tool, originally developed by John Boyd, a military strategist in the United States Air Force, to help fighter pilots during air combat who may possess less than perfect decision-making data (Luft, 2020).

The ideology behind the OODA loop is that you will outsmart the competition if you can adapt to changes in the environment *faster* than the competition. The OODA loop steps are:

Observe. This phase is about gathering information and understanding the internal and external environments, i.e. your operating context. As data is constantly changing, the assumption is that you must collect data as quickly as possible and make your decisions based on it. It doesn't matter if the data is outdated because you can go through the loop repeatedly.

. . .

Orient. The *most* important step! Here, you analyze and make sense of your data. Many factors such as past experiences, surveys, new information, and even genetics influence how you make decisions.

Decide. Among all the options generated, you have to *decide* which is the best course of action that will help you reach your objective.

Act. This is the final stage for implementing your hypothesis, either fully or in a test mode. As you get feedback from the environment, the loop starts over, considering new data. By considering this action a test, you can generate quick findings!

If you are mindful of these differences, then it means that during the Orient phase, you will notice what triggered you and see how your mind will react to different responses—almost like running various scenarios through simulation software.

There are various ways to create space in the Orient part of this cycle before you decide on an action; you could take a few deep breaths; go for a walk, or ask for time out before delivering a response. Either way, the ultimate outcome between snapping (reacting) and a measured response could be life-changing. After all, we all know that in most situations, our initial anger fades away over time. And how many times have we regretted the things that we said? Especially in relationships?

If you create a *pause* before responding to a negative trigger—this certainly does not indicate indecisiveness—it can assist tremendously with creating a positive outcome to a situation. A way to do this is by way of a methodology characterized by the acronym *PLACE*:

(P)ause. Take a deep breath when you experience the trigger. Whether it is something someone said or did.

(L)abel. Label, or give a tag—to your reaction. How are you feeling? Think back to what we said about your mind and feelings having to be in sync? Are you angry, frustrated, etc.?

(A)sk why. Ask yourself why you were triggered? Is it the event itself, or is it some association with something else in the back of your mind? Maybe it's associated with something that happened long ago. Is it rational that an occurrence like this triggers you? Was the event accidental or intentional?

(C)hoose. What is a skillful response? How important is what happened in the greater scheme of things? Alpha males do not let themselves get distracted from their goals by insignificant details. This is the part where you decide what you are going to do.

(E)mpower yourself. Learn the lesson from that specific situation–from the way you responded. If you often act in this way, you will develop muscle memory of response over reaction–of always doing the correct thing. The more you practice being calm and rational (in other words, being non-reactive), the more you respond, the better at it you become.

Most of us have reacted often in previous engagements with others because the human brain runs on auto-pilot most of the time! We have become *conditioned* by our life experiences. We all have a perceptual screen that we have built up over the years that allows certain stimuli in and keeps those that do not fit our perspective of life out. If we get faced with stimuli that we do not agree with, we suffer from cognitive bias. It is an unhappy feeling, and we naturally try to get out of the situation as soon as we can—often by reacting! (Rothstein, 2021). Viktor Frankl once said:

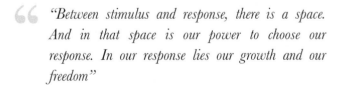 *"Between stimulus and response, there is a space. And in that space is our power to choose our response. In our response lies our growth and our freedom"*

The alpha male knows that he has a choice in

stressful situations about whether to react or respond. And that he cannot do both simultaneously (Eisler, 2018).

How to Communicate With Alphas in Business

Because alphas represent almost 70% of all executives, it is important to know their communication preferences. Even though you are reading this book to become an alpha male, once you reach those lofty heights, it is natural that you will have to engage more frequently with other alphas. Therefore, this list is both a guideline and a warning, as not all of the traits exhibited here are necessarily desirable.

Firstly though, let's look at some common characteristics amongst alphas within the corporate environment:

Not Desirable traits to be cautious of:

- **Expectations for High-performance levels** —They take high levels of performance for granted, not only in themselves but also in others. In their minds - excellent performance is often merely a basic expectation for everyone, not an achievement.
- **Process information fast**—They think and process information very fast - sometimes without listening well; they think

they know beforehand how an argument will end.

- **Impatience**—They can be very impatient. The desire to get shit done can sometimes lead to hasty decisions.
- **Big picture orientation**—They are generally not detail-oriented individuals.
- **Opinionated**—They can be very opinionated and will rarely admit to being wrong because they believe in the power of their own first impressions.
- **Intuitive**—Because they rely on their intuition to a great extent, they often feel justified being overly critical of others and don't always need a particular reason to act in such a way.
- **Directive**—The more pressurized an alpha becomes, the more he becomes directive and less involved in teamwork.
- **Dismissive**—They can be dismissive of those who cannot control their emotions and generally feel that emotions do not have a place at work.
- **Performance under pressure**—The more authority alphas get, i.e., the higher up in the organizations they go, the more pressure they experience and the greater the potential for pronounced mistakes. An alpha can sometimes be very harsh on himself, and therefore, he can be very harsh on others too. Especially, when he believes someone

underperforming can affect his own performance.

Now, there are good and bad traits, and as alphas, it is important to be sensitive to some of these characteristics, especially when dealing with people and their emotions. How then should we engage with other alphas?

Desirable traits to work with:

- **Be direct**—Alphas don't beat about the bush and don't appreciate people who do. Even if he may not like what you are saying, he will still appreciate your honesty.
- **Do not grovel**—Alphas are highly intelligent and see through this at once. This can be the difference between establishing a good working relationship or an irrelevant one. It can be difficult to navigate because alphas expect deference!
- **Give them data, stats, and facts**—The best way to get their attention is with lots and lots of credible data, preferably graphically depicted.
- **Be active**—Alphas cannot stand passivity.
- **Be practical**—Because he is practical and driven to achieve results - if you can show him a more straightforward way to produce fast results, he will typically go for it.

- **Arouse his curiosity**—Alphas are naturally curious. To establish an effective report, engage this curiosity and his instinct to compete.

- **Keep it short**—They hate long presentations, so keep it short. If choose to give them a long presentation, they will read ahead and start interrupting you.

- **Be balanced**—They tend to hate unconstructive criticism, so it's best to give balanced, useful critical feedback!

- **Be careful with praise**—Because alphas are self-validating (see chapter 5), they can sometimes feel uncomfortable both giving and receiving praise. At the same time, they do not want to appear soft. Be sensitive to the fact, therefore, that much of their conversation will contain critical comments.

- **Understand his bias against people-pleasing**—Since the alpha is not keen on being seen as a people-pleaser (also in chapter 5), he will worry that people will equate praise with people-pleasing or manipulation. It is important to understand this and where his critical bias comes from.

Do you want others to see these characteristics in you as an alpha? I would say yes *and* no. Be mindful of how people may perceive you - this is not the same as seeking validation. Accept accountability for your people's actions, accept criticism, and be aware of people's emotions. Everyone is not like you—thank goodness! If everyone in an organization was an alpha male, there would probably be constant conflict.

Summary

The key to confidence is understanding yourself and then believing in yourself! Self-worth is important and bears a drastic impact on your newly created beliefs and values, including your motivation to live by them!

There is a certain enigmatic presence when it comes to the dating world when you can be assertive without being arrogant about it! You've got the ability to use the *greater yang* divine energy to your advantage by applying it in your daily life and oozing masculinity that will help you ace your goals by being assertive, goal-focussed, accomplished, and dominant (in the right way!).

Confident alphas are *many* things! However, some things they are most certainly not are:

- A dick
- Someone that does not take care of their shit!
- Require validation from others
- They don't gossip or stalk chicks on social media

Alphas can conquer their fears in the right way by acknowledging them and taking appropriate action! An alpha also thinks before he responds and doesn't just react—because...Why? Because he is in control at *all* times.

When it comes to the corporate world, alphas in business are known to possess both desirable and undesirable traits—now you know what to look out for and how to handle the corporate alphas!

They also know that they don't have to embark on people-pleasing shenanigans to impress others, mainly because they have an internal locus of control. As an alpha, it is important to understand how alphas communicate—*both* the negative and positive sides of it! Be sensitive to the negative issues and about how people may perceive your interactions with them.

5

The Others – The Dangerous Need to Please Others and Its Origins

Why We Do It

What are the typical signs that you are a people-pleaser? Here are a few warning signs:

- You just *can't* stand saying 'no' to anyone to let people down—this happens often. You feel responsible for the happiness of others.
- A tendency to become resentful—because you can't say no. You work hard at helping others, and you start to despise those very same people.
- Lying—You tell lies to dodge uncomfortable situations that could lead to conflict.
- The constant need to fit in—regardless of the consequences.
- You apologize—a lot!
- Feeling guilty—often.

- You feel abused—you have a *feeling* that
  people misuse you and walk all over you.

A true alpha is not narcissistic, but he knows his self-worth; he is very assertive, outspoken, and does not live to please others. However, if you are exhibiting these signs, then it is clear that some part of you just cannot stand *not* being loved or wanted. This is often the result of an individual's upbringing.

Although pleasing people might *seem* like a good character trait, there are all kinds of inherent dangers in it. Truth be told, a people-pleaser is a liar. They do this for various reasons, with the most common being they want to fit in at any price. Often this is the result of some (negative) past experience.

Maybe an unloving parent triggered their need for love and acceptance. Or it could have been that if they disagreed with a parent or a sibling, then they would be on the receiving end of *significant* punishment. In order to avoid a repeat of that – they learned to lie. They try to please, although they may be resenting the individual whom they are trying to please.

It is a survival mechanism, and again, it is a self-fulfilling prophecy in action. The more the pleaser *exhibits* this type of behavior, the more ingrained it becomes until it is an absolute part of their being. They do not know any other way!

This is *not* the alpha male way. And although it may also not be the way of most beta males, it is true to say that betas are more susceptible to this.

Why We Need To Stop Pleasing People!

Pleasing people at *any* cost can be very detrimental to our relationships and, eventually, our health. Not to mention our careers. Some specific examples are:

- **Health problems.** Because your inner self is constantly at odds with how you are acting, it can lead to stress, exhaustion, hypertension, and other health-related problems.
- **Manipulation.** When people see that you cannot say *no*, they can abuse this and manipulate you!
- **Promotion.** Your boss is likely to see that you are a people-pleaser quickly. Although a nice 'asset' to have around –this is not the type of person that is *likely* to get promoted. So, you are likely to be left languishing in some menial job for a long period of time.
- **True colors.** People may start to dislike you because they cannot see your true colors; they don't know where they stand with you or who you actually are! It makes it hard for others to relate to you.
- **Stress.** Because you are always over-committed, you have no time for *yourself*. You need to DO YOU!

These symptoms and issues may manifest in the following types of real-life scenarios:

•Sometimes, people lie at work about their upbringing because they are scared that they will no longer be socially acceptable if they tell the truth about how poor they were.

•Some women accept marriage proposals from men they do not really love *just* because they feel they cannot or do not know how to say no! Some women go through with the marriage simply because they don't want to hurt the mens' feelings or out of fear of sitting on the shelves and having 12 cats! #crazycatlady

•In more unfortunate circumstances, doctors may not share bad news about a diagnosis with patients because they just cannot bear to divulge the information. Being the bearer of bad news can be a *heavy* burden, and even for trained professionals, this can become *too* much!

How to Stop It

This is just another *bad* habit that *can* be stopped. Revisit the section on creating habits to see what needs to be done. The first step is to become aware and accept that you have a problem. But you also need to understand the root causes of your behavior. So, you can do the "Why-Why" exercise on yourself, as discussed in Chapter 3. To aid you - here is a thread of ways to identify and address any potential issues:

Know that you have a desire to please. Think about your feelings when you get asked to do something.

Is it because you are scared of rejection that you are about to agree to whatever it is? Or is it because you want to fit in? *Understand* the emotions!

Start by saying 'no' to some simple requests that will not be detrimental to the person who asked it. No need to explain yourself. Just "No. I can't do that today." It will be uncomfortable at first. Get used to it!

Ask yourself about your assumptions and where they come from. Play a psychiatrist with your-self. Become curious about why you have a seeming inability to refuse to do something. Try to go back and analyze the origins of your behavior and then try to understand whether it makes sense. Do people that you work with today know about your past? Do they even care? So, why should you care about what they think?

Make a commitment—to tell the truth. This is one of your goals. Now use the techniques that I showed you and work out your long-term plan for saying *'no.'*

Don't be scared of the outcome. Saying no to something almost never has a fallout as bad as you think it will be - mainly because people are not thinking about you as often as you *think* they do. Harsh, but true!

. . .

Reconsider who deserves your time. Ask yourself whom you really want to help. Which friend or family member. At work, does everyone who approaches you deserve your time? What will the result be if you say no?

Realize that you can't please everyone. Nor should you have to. You can get hurt in the process, but at the same time, other people also have a responsibility to sort their own problems out. So in many respects, you may be doing a person a favor by saying 'no.' You are helping them develop themselves.

Remember that you can stop being a people-pleaser and still be a nice person. In fact, you will be more appreciated!

Rewire Your Brain—To Hell With Seeking Validation!

Validation and people-pleasing are like an *oxymoron*—but we need to steer clear of the morons! They are very closely related but *not* quite the same. Validation is not necessarily a bad thing; it is affirming and positive. It only becomes an issue when it is the focus of everything you do, and you're thirsting after it like a dog in heat, feeling like you need it from other people! There is a difference between being validated by others and self-validation.

So, what is the difference between validation and self-validation? Validation serves as recognition of someone else's behavior or experiences (the "atta-boy" if you will). Self-validation is when you recognize and acknowledge your *own* internal experiences. Validation is *not* important! Alpha males don't *need* it!

The alpha male can actively practice self-validation. The problem arises when, due to (normally) a lack of self-worth or self-esteem, a person cannot self-validate (or in the case of betas) may find validation from others to feel more important.

In life, our need for validation often comes from social media and how people have defined themselves in their profiles. A great deal of a beta's desire to be accepted and to be part of a group is now linked to social media, and it has, to a certain extent, fried their brains by fucking it in a non-sexy way! This is where you need to learn to unfuck yourself! By 'liking' a post, people are essentially *validating* each other. The more 'likes' the more validated and accepted they feel. Please tell me how Facebook likes equates to real-life benefits—I would really like to know the answer to this perplexing question!

You can probably already tell where I am going with this. This type of validation and the need for validation in-person can have serious negative consequences on a person's feelings of self-worth. When a beta does not hear praise or acceptance, he conditioned himself to - it can lead to low self-worth, anxiety, and even depression.

To break this beta-type cycle of behavior, you would need to do a number of things—these are more healthy, new habits to cultivate:

. . .

Understand the behavior. Do you feel that you need validation through social media? Learning to recognize when you need external validation is an important first step. No matter how embarrassed you might think it to be now, but if you try to Tetris through life, you are going to fucking disappear!

Take a break from social media. In this way, you will start to care less about how people respond to your posts. Although it may be difficult at first, it is *not* impossible. And you will feel less stressed about what people think of your posts and hence of you. Take up some other forms of activity or sport. Team sport is a great way to get external validation in a constructive manner! Nothing like a *Hoo-rah* from your teammates for a boost!

Track your progress. As we showed with developing new habits, it is important to track your progress and see how you are getting on by keeping a journal. Be ready to praise or realign yourself as may be required. If you are not the journaling type, keep a short list of tasks/checkpoints on your phone and tick it off as you progress!

Don't ask for validation. Alpha males ask themselves first whether they have done a good job. *Not* others! You are not Lassie; you don't need a treat and to be petted.

· · ·

Make peace with yourself. Recognize who you are and cultivate a harmonious relationship with yourself. Understand that you are enough and what you are doing is enough. There is no need for external praise. You need to be zen and gel with yourself—you know—karma your own shit!

Don't rely on instant gratification. This is another problem with social media. Ninety percent of the people that 'like' your posts may have never even met you. They don't *know* you! So, how can their opinions really mean anything? Just be yourself and remember that you are not defined by the opinions of others—good or bad (JLO, 2020)

An alpha male does not crave external validation. When he gets it he acknowledges it and moves on. In his heart, he knows whether it was a job well done or not. He doesn't carry on seeking it by asking, "Do you REALLY think what I did was good?" **insert *Puss in Boots Face*** (Gaba, 2019).

Learning to Set Boundaries. Alpha males know how to set boundaries. Whether this is by saying 'no' firmly when approached for help (when appropriate to do so) or in relationships with women. Even though many important things make a relationship work (like trust, commitment, and respect), if there are no clear boundaries, it is going to be a bumpy road in the relationship ahead. If you can't set boundaries straight away, the day you decide to finally put your foot down, people will take a fence...LOL! See what I did there? (Can't seem to resist a dad joke here and there).

Why does a person set boundaries? Simply to keep themselves from being *abused*. From being pushed around like a shopping cart! And let's face it—that is not the type of guy that women respect, especially not in the long run, *and no one likes a shopping cart with fucked up wheel alignment!*

There are two reasons why beta males do not set boundaries for others—they feel guilty if they do, and/or they are afraid of the outcome or the result if they do implement these limits. So, they muddle along. Not setting boundaries is another form of people-pleasing. Trust me, acting like *that* - you will never be a hit!

Setting boundaries is a healthy thing to do. It makes it clear to you and your partner—or people at work, for that matter—what your tolerance levels are and what the implications are for overstepping those boundaries.

It makes you an assertive alpha male, *not* someone who is aggressive or who should be feared. In fact, the consequences of not setting boundaries are generally worse than setting them. It will leave you powerless, and people will not respect you! You don't want to be like an aggressive wolf who practices love at first bite—especially when it comes to dating!

To set healthy boundaries in a relationship, you must know yourself. You should know which things you stand for and which you don't—the things that people should respect you for. It is yet another habit-forming goal, by the way.

Then, once you have formulated your boundaries, you have to let your partner know what they are. Not necessarily by sitting her down and giving her a lecture called "My Boundaries," but if she oversteps a boundary, you have to explain why you don't like it and why you consider it to be one of your *no-go's*.

Let me give you another example - perhaps career-related. If someone at works rubs you the wrong way or is simply rude to you, the best thing to do is to ask them to speak privately and explain that disrespect will not be tolerated, and if it continues, it is going to be a problem. Be tactful and explain that you want to build a productive relationship and would appreciate it if the person came to you directly and in private if they ever have an issue with you. They will respect you for standing up for yourself and appreciate it even more that you have done it in private - it shows that you really mean it when you say you wanna make it work. On the other hand, if you decide to go for a "public display of power" - prepare for retaliation and a new enemy. Using the diplomatic approach, I had forged some of the strongest alliances in the past. Those who had seemed to be threatened by my assertiveness and ambition in the beginning - had eventually become some of my closest collaborators.

You have to be realistic when you formulate your boundaries—they cannot be too tight or too slack. Too tight, and it will seem as if your standards are unbelievably high and even obsessively so. Too slack, and it will seem like there are no boundaries. Think of it in athletic terms–when athletes jump over a hurdle, it is hard, but not impossible!

The main thing about sustaining boundaries is that once they have been set in a relationship, it is OK to walk away from the relationship if your partner keeps goofing them up. It shows that she has no respect for you, and the relationship is doomed to fail anyway.

Don't expect immediate results when setting boundaries. It is a process to develop and maintain your boundaries, and you should see it in that light. As with your other goals, don't get too upset if you don't get it right immediately. Keep your journal and learn the lessons so that you can improve.

A further issue with letting people transgress your boundaries is that you may end up bottling up your emotions until it blows up like a bottle of diet Coca-Cola when Mentos are added to it (don't try it at home)! Then it is a reaction–not a response! There are ways to set boundaries without hurting people. If people tend to walk into your office all the time, you can tell them that you are unfortunately only available for social conversations during your lunch break due to your commitments.

Setting boundaries means becoming more assertive. Be mindful that being assertive is not the same as being aggressive. Assertiveness is about respectfully expressing yourself about what you want. It is a communication skill that can contribute to building your confidence. Some of the benefits of being assertive are:

· · ·

Decreasing conflict. When you set boundaries and communicate assertively, you are bound to be faced with less conflict as people will begin to respect you and realize that you cannot be pushed around. So not *Fight Club*–quite the opposite!

Making you more comfortable. People are as comfortable as an old shoe in an environment where they are liked and like others. And because you are an assertive alpha male who people know they can look up to and trust, being assertive enhances that and makes everyone around you more at ease by being in your presence.

Developing confidence. Being assertive grows your confidence and feelings of self-worth, especially if what you say is based on facts. The positive feedback that you constantly get from your environment is likely to grow this confidence.

Promoting your self-esteem. If your self-esteem is high, then it promotes your confidence, and you see things and people in a different light. It encourages the way you interact with them and makes you more self-assured.

· · ·

Releasing your time and mind. Much like with people-pleasing—when you become assertive, stand up for yourself, and set boundaries—you suddenly have more peace of mind because you don't feel abused anymore.

Developing respect for yourself and others. Assertively letting others know how you feel about things will create more respect for you as a person. Additionally, with a calm sort of assertiveness, you start to see other people more as human beings, and over time you develop respect for them and their feelings.

Learning to Manage Your Stress

Throughout this book, I emphasize the need to manage your stress properly—both from a mental and physical health perspective. This is so important that I need to provide some additional advice on this matter because if you cannot manage your stress levels, you will never reach the alpha male peak—you don't attempt *Mount Everest* to only get to Base 2!

Leaf (2021) developed a process called *neuro cycling* to help people deal with stress, especially stress episodes of an acutely traumatic nature. It is a five-step process that works as follows:

Gather—You harvest and collect information about your thoughts and emotions. Just become aware of what they are and how they are making you feel. Although you should consciously go through this you shouldn't spend too much time on it. For example, you have just heard that a family member was involved in a serious auto accident. First, you become aware of feelings of fear, anger, and concern. Then, you find out the details of the accident. This process already makes you calmer and more in control of the situation.

Reflect—You take the time to learn deeply and intentionally. There are three sub-activities involved here:

- Ask yourself what has happened—the who, what, where, and how.
- Answer yourself by reviewing the information that you receive
- Discuss the information with yourself while you look for additional information. Go through it and try to logically address each particular point.

Write—This involves writing down the information that you have now analyzed, albeit superficially so. Your brain has had time to reflect. Now it is 'seeing' its reflections on paper. This, in turn, reinforces and strengthens your thinking process.

Recheck—It is a simple but highly effective process to intentionally go through everything you have written down to make sure that it makes sense. You must first *understand* in order to learn. So, make sure you understand what you wrote, check whether it is logically arranged and whether there is sufficient information to draw some semblance of sense from it.

Active Reach—Explain what you are learning out loud —to yourself or anyone or anything within reach. Actively 'reteach' the information in a way as if you are teaching another person something completely new. Look from the outside in, at what you are doing as if you are watching a movie. Look for bits of information or images that bring back the information to your mind's eye.

This process of building your brain during times of stress will help you develop a robust ability to handle stress and will ensure that the negative impacts of stress are reduced.

Summary

People-pleasing is a type of survival mechanism that a person most often learns from their caregivers at a young age—normally to avoid conflict. However, the conflict eventually manifests within yourself. The more a people-pleaser does this, the more ingrained this type of behavior becomes in their psyche.

I've shown that there are many inherent dangers in such behavior, ranging from potential health issues to stress-related problems, such as rejection by colleagues and a host of other issues. I also showed that people-pleasing is a bad habit that can be kicked! Most importantly, you need to understand the root causes of the behavior. And contrary to what many people-pleasers might think—you can still be an alpha that is *nice* and valued by people without indulging in this kind of behavior.

Closely related to the issue of people-pleasing is *validation*. An alpha male does not crave external validation. He is an expert at self-validation, setting boundaries, and getting others to respect these boundaries. He knows that boundaries are important to earn respect, especially when it comes to relationships with women.

Lastly—it is important to manage your stress levels if you want to reach the alpha male peak. You will not be able to function properly in pursuing your strategy to reach your goals and purpose if you are sidetracked by issues related to stress.

6

Connected People-Connected Strategy

I wrote extensively on the underpinnings of why people are attracted to alphas, specifically about confidence and positive male energy. What is crucial here is to strengthen relationships with others, build meaningful rapports, and maintain them!

But how, specifically, do you forge these all-important relationships? Here are some guidelines.

Connect people

Networking is an impressive and important skill if you want to be recognized as a true alpha. If you can introduce people with like-minded pursuits to each other, it shows that you are interested in them as people and that they matter.

If you know of someone with a specific skill that can benefit someone else—introduce them! Such a symbiotic process is part of growing that self-confidence, which will result in you showing positive masculine energy.

I often introduce business owners to each other if I think the connection would benefit both sides. More often than not, both parties are immensely grateful for the help in advancing THEIR goals and ambitions. You should not expect anything in return; however, people tend to remember the good deeds, and most will look for ways to repay the favor! E.g. In many cases, my clients were finding new clients for me by referring their partner businesses and professional connections in their attempts to balance the scales.

Furthermore, playing a "matchmaker" will also develop your communication skills if you are a bit shy or introverted. This is, in fact, one of the best ways to go about nurturing your ability to meet new people without making it look artificial. After all, you have a purpose in talking to this individual!

Take them with you. If you have an invite to a special occasion, why not invite one of the people in your network along? This kills two birds with one stone —you are showing you care, and you will get to know the person better. It could even turn into a date! The possibilities are limitless! *(wink-wink, nudge-nudge)*.

Use 'we'. People tend to be put off by people who use 'I' too much. This is a relatively quick fix to build rapport with other people and to develop your team at work. The more you use 'we,' the more people get a feeling of togetherness. It also shows that you are a team player and someone who cares for his people. This is actually one of the primary leadership techniques that officers get taught very early in their careers in the military.

Delegate. An alpha allows others to feel empowered by trusting them with certain tasks that demand responsibility–it saves time for the self-assured male and makes others feel good that the alpha has entrusted *them* to perform the task!

However, it bears saying that you as the alpha need to ensure that you delegate tasks in a mindful manner– meaning to the right person and then following up where and when needed–after all, you are ultimately accountable for the task to get done. Efficiently!

Be on time. A relatively easy to implement habit is to always be on time or to deliver whatever you are supposed to, in a timeous manner. People easily get a reputation for tardiness if they are always late.

You may think it happens only once or twice, but if you carefully analyze your life, you will notice a pattern if you are prone to this *bad* habit. More importantly— others will as well! Being on time also says that you are dependable. There is nothing more irritating than someone who is always late for a meeting. This is not the alpha way.

I am not even sure where I picked this up, but my expectation for myself is:

- If you are early = You're on time
- If you're on time = You're late
- If you are late = Don't even bother

Dress properly. Yet another easy, quick win. We spoke about this in Chapter 1. A person who is always neatly dressed is someone who catches the eye. Remember— "You can never be overdressed or overeducated" (Oscar Wilde). What does this mean? Well, simply that you can never look too good or be too smart. If you go to a function and don't know what the dress code is, dress formally. If you arrive there and see that it is an informal event, you can always take off your jacket and tie. If it is the other way around and you do not have a jacket with you, then you have a problem!

Treat people with respect. This is not people-pleasing. If you treat the doorman with the same courtesy as you do your boss, people will notice. But there is a more nuanced aspect to this. When you start treating people at all levels with respect, it impacts you at a deeper psychological level, positively influencing your self-respect. And more self-respect =*more* self-confidence!

Don't disagree with others just on principle. Be

prepared to have an open mind when someone else has a genuinely good idea, applaud it, and be ready to support it. If a compromise can be reached between your viewpoint and that of others, it is best to do it in most cases. Be careful not to want to "win" at any cost.

By your friends, you will be known. It is a well-worn cliché, but it's true nonetheless. People tend to associate you in their minds with the people that you hang out with. So, choose *wisely*! People will only respect you if they know that you surround yourself with like-minded people of high integrity.

Listen rather than talk. We all know *that guy* that, when you talk to them—is always looking away or at their watch or phone and hardly ever looks you in the eye. The first and foremost skill of having a conversation is showing that you care about the person and the topic at hand. Active listening means that you engage the person with your eyes, positive body language, and ask questions to show that you are *focused*.

Inquire about people's well-being. When you see people, inquire about their well-being and of their family's. You will be amazed at how quickly people respond positively to you the next time they see you! Being all frosty and business-like is not always pleasant to everyone–so let that shit go! Some people are much more sensitive to this type of inquiry than others, but everyone appreciates it when an alpha asks them about their well-being.

Remember small details. It is always impressive when you ask someone about something they had told you previously, especially if it relates to their private life or family members. Perhaps it was a wife that was ill. Asking after her well-being by name will elicit positive emotional responses.

If you don't feel like you can trust your memory on this, you may even keep a simple diary of people's details that you update every time you engage with someone. Forgetting someone's name after being introduced is a *no-no*! There are easy tricks to remember names, but the simplest is to repeat the person's name in your mind a few times once you have been introduced and then make some sort of association with something else.

Let's say the guy's name is Ben. You may respond as follows, "Ben? Ben? Oh, yes, I know a Ben from Brooklyn. He runs a small shop there." And then you may think of Big Ben, the clock tower in London, to try and make some sort of association. The next time you run into that person, the Big Ben clock should jump up in your mind's eye.

· · ·

Admit your mistakes. I mentioned that alphas are ready to apologize when they make mistakes. People do not take this as a weakness but rather see it as a positive character trait. Once you have admitted your mistake, explain what you are going to do to fix it.

Ask for feedback. This is not the same as validation. In order to grow, you need to get constant feedback on your performance—especially as you move along the path to reaching your goals. Do not wait till a mistake is made for this to be done. The purpose of soliciting feedback is to prevent mistakes from happening in the first place. People generally respond positively to this. Feedback can be requested from anyone that you are involved with—not only peers.

Provide feedback. If receiving feedback is important for your growth, then obviously, providing constructive feedback is important for the growth and development of others! Positive criticism is essential, but it needs to be done *properly*. An alpha does this by setting the scene appropriately and telling the person beforehand the purpose of the conversation, balancing between areas for improvement, and recognizing the positive aspects. Address the issue and the behavior—not the person!

Be proactive. It is always a good thing to try and anticipate your boss's next move or request. If you are proactive, it shows that you're committed and think ahead. This approach will only propel you further as you will be known as the guy who always seems to be one step ahead of everyone else. As you get positive feedback from this, it will enhance your confidence and masculine energy, which will make you more *attractive* to others! Not that you should care, but you are also likely to encounter those who feel threatened by it as you are setting a whole new level of standard that others may feel the need to live up to.

Have your own mind. An alpha male is known to be a leader. And a leader does *not* get upset by everyone else's opinions. You have to be able to speak your mind on a subject, whether in support or disagreement. People do not respect someone who always follows the pack or popular opinion!

Don't gossip. You should spend time with people socializing and getting to know them. When the conversation turns to gossip, gently steer it away, or if there is no other option—then eject yourself from the conversation. As an alpha on your way to achieving great things, you don't have time to speculate about the lives of others. Gossips and greatness do not go hand in hand.

Don't waste people's time. Get more respect by showing people you respect their time. What does this mean? Don't ask questions you can answer yourself, don't plan meetings that you don't need, and don't take forever getting back to people.

Have *proper* meetings. Badly run, or unnecessary meetings are another example of wasting people's time. Most people don't like meetings, so make sure it is worth their while to attend. No regular meeting should ever be longer than 45 minutes. If you take any longer, you will notice people's attention falter and potentially completely disappear halfway through. Have a proper agenda and structure the meeting well. Most importantly, make sure the meeting has a purpose.

Never acknowledge "defeat". Don't say "I don't know." If you are caught on the spot, just say, "I will need to look into this and get back to you". Alternatively, work together to figure it out or point the person in the *right* direction. Don't let the person leave empty-handed. They should at least be endowed with more knowledge than when they approached you for assistance!

Understand how others like to work. COVID-19 has given the world a reset regarding work practices. But despite the advantages of tools like Zoom, many people still prefer face-to-face interaction. Others like to communicate via email. Although you cannot be everything to everyone, there are ways to try and accommodate diverse requirements.

First and foremost, this means engaging the people around you about how they feel and what their preferences are. You won't be able to accommodate everyone, but at least they will see your efforts. People *don't* expect alphas to be wizards!

Train, don't punish. Yes, Mr. Grey–curb your enthusiasm! Show that you care for people by teaching them the ropes and helping them fix and learn from their mistakes. Give people every chance to grow - if anything, it is an opportunity to groom the person into a helpful ally.

Manage upward. This may be tricky at first, but an alpha lets his boss know what he needs to get the job done. Make it clear that you will do a great job if you are given the resources you need. In a corporate environment, be prepared to compromise and explain the rationale behind the requests.

Champion your people. Why not use your personal goal-setting techniques to help your employees develop and grow theirs. Understand what they want to achieve and then help them set their goals and create new worthwhile habits. Having successful subordinates speaks well about an alpha's leadership abilities. Furthermore, on many occasions, by standing up for your people, you significantly boost your status.

Following the techniques I have given you, you can propel your personal brand and your career to unexpected heights. Become a people's champion and reap the rewards.

Conclusion-The Incremental Model For Success!

How To Tie It All Together

There is an important consideration: You don't develop yourself to become an alpha male *solely* to get the 'target.'! You first become an alpha male, and as a result, you have the *ability* to get your' target.' It's a subtle but important difference.

In this book, I have presented you with an abundance of strategies and techniques to develop your mindset into an alpha male mentality. I am not suggesting you do everything on the list - each person is unique and different things work better for different people. What I do want to highlight - is that you need to mix-and-match my suggestions to formulate your overall strategy and approach. My suggestion is to use my IMS model.

The Incremental Model for Success

Everything I have written in this book underpins what I call *The Incremental Model for Success (IMS)* which, in other words, is a sort of strategic plan towards success. This model consists of four elements: *Foundational Pillars*, the *Supportive Ecosystem*, the *Inner Core*, and the *Inputs*. Note that these things are not sequential. They work more like an ecosystem!

The IMS could be compared to a house. The *Foundation Pillars* are the keystones keeping the whole house structurally sound. The walls, ceilings, and the floor would represent the *Supportive ecosystem*. Some of them may not be essential for survival; however, would you want to live in a house with no walls or no roof?

Thirdly, *the core* is the content of the house—all the things that make it a home rather than just a house - both physical and not (e.g. warmth, decor, your huge ass TV, etc.). Finally, *the inputs* are building materials that allow you to rebuild and reshape the house to your liking—perhaps expanding or upscaling, or perhaps demolishing and rebuilding.

Let us cover each element of the model in more detail. This model is your practical strategy for becoming an alpha male.

Inner Core. Let's start from inside the house. The inner core of the model is your purpose- the foundational principle that *drives* you and where self-actualization happens. It is that fire inside you that forces you to *not* settle for the mediocre. In order to accomplish your purpose, you have to work through your *Supportive Ecosystem*, which, in turn, rests on the *Foundational Pillars*.

Your *Inner core* is boosted by understanding what a true alpha is, how he behaves, and the difference between being an alpha vs. an *asshole* "bad boy". You reach the point of self-realization when you understand the traits affecting your professional development and your personal brand and even the traits that scare women away. You've learned to dig deep within yourself and practice mindfulness to enhance your self-aware-ness—creating calm and serene confidence!

Foundational Pillars. Your foundational pillars are the four cornerstones that keep the alpha males sane and in the lead:

1. **The Pillar of Resilience** (Mental resilience, drive to never give up, learning from failures, ...)
2. **The Pillar of Intelligence** (Self-development, emotional intelligence, personal growth, ...)
3. **The Pillar of Leadership** (Confidence, Assertiveness, Care for others, Meaningful connections, ...)
4. **The Pillar of Fulfillment** (The joys of life, Self-actualization, the rewards of the lifestyle you lead, the feeling of accomplishment, belonging, ...)

If you take away even just *one* of the cornerstones, the integrity of the house is compromised. Sure, the house might not collapse right away, but the walls will be cracking and the floor shaking. An alpha that intends to continue his alpha male lifestyle will need to maintain these four *wholesome* cornerstones by leading a balanced and fulfilling life.

Supportive Ecosystem. Your supportive ecosystem is all about being self-disciplined, learning from past mistakes, and forming new habits that will best serve you! In the house analogy, the supportive ecosystem is a set of walls, floors, and ceilings that protect you from the wind, rain, and other noise that otherwise would distract you from your real purpose. Essentially, it is the habits that you nurture, the people surrounding you, and the environment you place yourself in–all working in your favor or against it. Don't forget–healthy walls are what keeps the house warm.

Inputs. Your actions–they form a bundle of materials for you to continue perfecting that house of yours. The *better* the actions–the better the building materials. As mentioned earlier, you are the CEO of your life (aka *this* house).

Tear the *fucking* walls down if you need to expand, get rid of the furniture that is in the way or does not work with the house's overall interior (e.g. toxic people, time-wasting habits, etc.). You are also always welcome to repaint the walls a different color (e.g. change your direction if your life goals have evolved into something new).

The dangers are the faulty materials for building: pleasing people or seeking validation, etc. Such materials may temporarily plug some holes but render the house vulnerable and poorly insulated in the long run! They can help alleviate the symptoms of loneliness and low self-worth, but the relief is very temporary (instant gratification vs. delayed gratification) as it does not solve the underlying problem.

My Parting Words to You - Arise the New Alpha

The IMS model works! Step by step, drop by drop–the incremental changes accumulate to *great* things! I have applied it in my own life with great *success*. This is why my confidence levels are where they are today and why people are attracted to me.

As I said right at the beginning of the book, there is *no* quick fix for becoming an alpha male. You have to work at it every day, but it becomes progressively easier as your image and your vision grow closer together.

The reading purist may ask—but why did you not start the book with the IMS model? There is a very specific reason for this—I wanted you to first read through the whole book to get an overall feel of what being an alpha male is all about and not fixate on the specific sections as they relate to the IMS.

The real work starts now...but it is very important to remember that the changes are best done in small increments as it doesn't shock the system as much, and we are more likely to *permanently* change our habits if the change is incremental!

Furthermore, as mentioned earlier, I have a lovely gift for you - a *FREE* ebook on achieving financial independence as a true alpha - download your free copy at modernalphabooks.com

You have now graduated as a newly morphed alpha, and I welcome you to the brotherhood! Rise! I can't wait for the next phase in our journey together! See you there!

***** P.S. I would be very grateful if you could please leave a review on Amazon to let me know if this guide worked for you and any success stories and experiences you have to share! *****

Just a reminder...

Thank you for joining the Alpha Fam! To show my gratitude I would like to give you a FREE gift!

9 Secret Ways to Financial Independence as A True Alpha

Claim yours at www.modernalphabooks.com

References

10 tips for being more goal-oriented at work. (n.d.). Indeed. https://www.indeed.com/career-advice/career-development/being-goal-oriented-at-work

16 effects of testosterone on the body. (2014, April 21). Healthline. https://www.healthline.com/health/low-testosterone/effects-on-body#Muscle

21 tips to stop being a people-pleaser. (2016, May 17). PsychCentral. https://psychcentral.com/lib/21-tips-to-stop-being-a-people-pleaser#3

Achor, S. (2015, July 2). *"What you think, you become."* SUCCESS. https://www.success.com/what-you-think-you-become/

Altman, I. (2017, August 22). *3 ways to make new habits stick.* Forbes. https://www.forbes.com/sites/ianaltman/2017/08/22/3-ways-to-make-new-habits-stick/?sh=4ec96535378a

Bose, R. (2021, February 4). *Using the domino effect in life.* Medium. https://medium.com/the-31-5-guy/using-the-domino-effect-in-life-ceb384083add

Bradberry, T. (2017, January 10). *10 things confident people don't do.* Entrepreneur. https://www.entrepreneur.com/article/287463

Brown, J. (2013, January 2). *10 reasons why your alpha personality will bring you success.* ADDICTED2SUCCESS. https://addicted2success.com/success-advice/10-reasons-why-your-alpha-personality-will-bring-you-success/

Castrillon, C. (2020a, January 26). *5 strategies to build unshakable self-confidence.* Forbes. https://www.forbes.com/sites/carolinecastrillon/2020/01/26/5-strategies-to-build-unshakable-self-confidence/?sh=39e6cf388c6f

Castrillon, C. (2020b, July 12). *5 ways to go from a scarcity to abundance mindset.* Forbes. https://www.forbes.com/sites/carolinecastrillon/2020/07/12/5-ways-to-go-from-a-scarcity-to-abundance-mindset/?sh=4b22a4b11197

Centeno, A. (2019, June 15). *10 quick tips to increase mens' confidence (build your self esteem).* Real Men Real Style. https://www.realmenrealstyle.com/mens-confidence/

Chauhan, H. (2016, February 11). *9 character differences between alpha male and a bad boy.* Alpha MALE. https://www.alphamale.co/difference-between-a-bad-boy-and-an-alpha-male/

Cook, A. (2020, June 11). *The danger of being a people pleaser.* Alison Cook, Ph.D. https://www.alisoncookphd.com/danger-of-being-a-people-pleaser/

Cutruzzula, K. (2020, January 27). *7 ways to regain your footing (and self-worth) after you disappoint yourself.* shine. https://advice.theshineapp.com/articles/7-ways-to-regain-your-footing-and-self-worth-after-you-disappoint-yourself/

Daskal, L. (2016, May 19). *7 powerful habits that make you more assertive.* Inc. https://www.inc.com/lolly-daskal/7-powerful-habits-that-make-you-more-assertive.html

Disco, E. (2021, February 26). *How to be a True Alpha Male.* APPROACH ANXIETY. https://approachanxiety.com/how-to-be-a-true-alpha-male/

Duszyński, M. (2021, March 8). *Pareto principle & the 80/20 rule.* ResumeLab.

Eisler, M. (2018, July 14). *Respond vs. react: How to keep your cool in times of stress.* MELISSA EISLER. https://melissaeisler.com/respond-vs-react-how-to-keep-your-cool-in-times-of-stress/

Gaba, S. (2019, July 24). *Stop seeking validation from others.* Psychology Today. https://www.psychologytoday.com/za/blog/addiction-and-recovery/201907/stop-seeking-validation-others

Gaining self confidence like an "alpha male". (n.d.). Death of a Wantrepreneur. http://www.judaborrayo.com/uncategorized/alphamale/

Greenawald, E. (2014, October 8). *42 ways to make sure people like you—and respect you.* Themuse; https://www.themuse.com/advice/42-ways-to-make-sure-people-like-youand-respect-you

Gunasekara, O. (n.d.). *Balancing cortisol, the stress hormone, in men.* BodyLogicMD. https://www.bodylogicmd.com/hormones-for-men/cortisol/

Haden, J. (2016, October 18). *86 ways to become incredibly successful.* Inc. https://www.inc.com/jeff-haden/everything-you-need-to-know-to-achieve-all-your-goals-9-ways-to-be-incredibly-su.html

How to be assertive without being aggressive. (2016, July 7). CABA. https://www.caba.org.uk/help-and-guides/information/how-be-assertive-without-being-aggressive

How to set healthy relationship boundaries. (n.d.). ALPHA MALE MENTALITY. https://www.alphamalementality.com/set-healthy-relationship-boundaries

Howse, C. (2016, October 7). *4 fears every guy's gotta face.* AVERAGE 2 ALPHA. https://average2alpha.com/4-fears-every-guys-gotta-face/

JLO. (2020, December 17). *Desperately seeking validation.* Medium. https://medium.com/change-becomes-you/desperately-seeking-validation-238f1db7c25c

Kaufman, S. B. (2015, December 10). *The myth of the alpha male.* Greater Good. https://greatergood.berkeley.edu/article/item/the_myth_of_the_alpha_male

Leaf, C. (2021). *Cleaning up your mental mess : 5 simple, scientifically proven steps to reduce anxiety, stress, and toxic thinking.* Baker Books.

Levy, B. R., Slade, M. D., Kunkel, S. R., & Kasl, S. V. (2002). *Longevity increased by positive self-perceptions of aging.* Journal of Personality and Social Psychology, *83*(2). https://doi.org/

Ludeman, K., & Erlandson, E. (2004, May 1). *Coaching the alpha male.* Harvard Business Review. https://hbr.org/2004/05/coaching-the-alpha-male

Luft, A. (2020, March 17). *The OODA loop and the half-beat.* The Strategy Bridge. https://thestrategybridge.org/the-bridge/2020/3/17/the-ooda-loop-and-the-half-beat

Luna, A. (2014, May 19). *How to become your own best friend.* LONERWOLF. https://lonerwolf.com/how-to-become-your-own-best-friend/

McKay, B. (2015, October 5). *Men and status: How testosterone fuels the drive for status.* The Art of Manliness. https://www.artofmanliness.com/articles/men-and-status-how-testosterone-affects-status/

McKay, B. (2018, April 17). *Finding fulfillment in a world obsessed with happiness.* The Art of Manliness. https://www.artofmanliness.com/articles/podcast-397-the-3-pillars-of-a-meaningful-life/

McKay, B. (2020, June 3). *A guide for the journey to your true calling.* The Art of Manliness. https://www.artofmanliness.com/articles/find-your-true-calling/

McKay, B., & McKay, K. (2015, December 18). *Men & status: Why you should care about your status.* The Art of Manliness. https://www.artofmanliness.com/articles/men-status-why-you-should-care-about-your-status/

Mcleod, S. (2020, December 29). *Maslow's hierarchy of needs.* Simply Psychology. https://www.simplypsychology.org/maslow.html#gsc.tab=0

Meah, A. (2019, December 16). *35 alpha male quotes on success.* AWAKEN THE GREATNESS WITHIN. https://www.awakenthegreatnesswithin.com/35-alpha-male-quotes-on-success/

Miller, K. D. (2021, May 19). *9 best self-esteem questionnaires (+Rosenberg self-esteem scale).* PositivePsychology.

https://positivepsychology.com/rosenberg-self-esteem-scale-questionnaires/

Morgan, K. (2018, August 14). *Why people pleasing is bad for you*. Life Labs. https://lifelabs.psychologies.co.uk/posts/37716-why-people-pleasing-is-bad-for-you

Murphy, S. (2015, September 16). *The Attractiveness of Confidence*. Society for Personality and Social Psychology. https://www.spsp.org/news-center/blog/romantic-confidence

Nuur, D. (2018, July 19). *Masculine and feminine energy - balancing masculine & feminine*. Goop. https://goop.com/wellness/spirituality/balancing-your-feminine-and-masculine-energies/

Oberoi, A. (2020, October 14). *9 practical ways to discipline yourself quickly*. Kool Stories. https://www.kool-stories.com/blog/practical-ways-to-discipline-yourself

Parekh, R. (2019, January 22). *8 benefits of standing up for yourself and being assertive*. RUCHI PAREKH. https://ruchiparekh.com/2019/01/22/8-benefits-of-standing-up-for-yourself-and-being-assertive/

Paulo Coelho. (2010). *The Winner Stands Alone*. (2nd ed.). Harper Collins Uk.

People-pleasing: And how to overcome It. (2018, February 8). THE SCHOOL of LIFE. https://www.theschooloflife.com/thebookoflife/people-pleasing-and-how-to-overcome-it/

Rosenthal, R. (2012). *THE ROSENTHAL EXPERIMENT*. Google. https://sites.google.com/site/7arosenthal/

Rothstein, L. (2021). *Space between stimulus and response*. University of Minnesota Extension. https://extension.umn.edu/two-you-video-series/space-between-stimulus-and-response

Sanders, K. (2015, September 23). *A Man's Guide to Finding True Purpose in Life*. THE GOOD MEN PROJECT. https://goodmenproject.com/featured-content/a-mans-guide-to-finding-true-purpose-in-life-dg/

Schwanke, C. (2017). *What colors do women prefer on men*. LOVEToKNOW; https://mens-fashion.loveto-know.com/What_Colors_Do_Women_Prefer_on_Men

Soh, R. (2017, August 18). *10 benefits of self-discipline*. Seek Five. https://seekfive.org/10-benefits-of-self-discipline/

The best exercises to increase testosterone. (n.d.). Piedmont Healthcare. https://www.piedmont.org/living-better/the-best-exercises-to-increase-testosterone

The pygmalion effect (Rosenthal effect) definition, example & summary! (2018, October 10). Jeroen de Flander. https://jeroen-de-flander.com/the-pygmalion-effect-leadership/

Unified Action. (2016, February 5). The Lightning Press. https://www.thelightningpress.com/unified-action/

Western, D. (2017, July 25). *How to become an alpha male & stop being a beta*. Wealthy GORILLA. https://wealthygo-rilla.com/become-alpha-male/

What is masculine energy? (2016, March 8). Meditate a CENTER for HEALING ARTS. https://www.medi-tatecenter.com/what-is-masculine-energy/

Why self-esteem is important and its dimensions. (2015). MentalHelp.net. https://www.mentalhelp.net/self-esteem/why-its-important/

Woronko, M. (2014, September 17). *8 reasons why your worst enemy is yourself*. Lifehack. https://www.lifehack.org/articles/communication/8-reasons-why-your-worst-enemy-yourself.html

Yaribeygi, H., Panahi, Y., Sahraei, H., Johnston, T. P., & Sahebkar, A. (2017). *The impact of stress on body function: A review*. EXCLI Journal, 16(1),. https://doi.org/

You are the CEO of your life. (n.d.). Personal Excellence. https://personalexcellence.co/blog/ceo/

Young, S. H. (2007, August 14). *18 tricks to make new habits stick*. Lifehack. https://www.lifehack.org/articles/featured/18-tricks-to-make-new-habits-stick.html

Printed in Great Britain
by Amazon